GAMES FOR GIR

BROWNIE SCOUTS
INTERMEDIATE GIRL SCOUTS
SENIOR GIRL SCOUTS

With a Few Suggestions
on
How to Select and Present a Game

GIRL SCOUTS
National Organization
155 East 44th Street
New York 17, N. Y.

Catalog No. 20-632, 35 cents

COPYRIGHT, 1942
BY GIRL SCOUTS

PRINTED IN THE UNITED STATES OF AMERICA

ACKNOWLEDGMENTS

THIS NEW EDITION of the *Girl Scout Game Book* includes many new games that have proved interesting to Girl Scouts.

The book is in no sense complete and no effort has been made to present numberless excellent games that are available in other volumes. It seeks only to give some of the games that have proved best for various Girl Scout occasions, and to pass along some of the adaptations the girls themselves have made. It is hoped that leaders and Girl Scouts will continue to send to National Headquarters new games or variations of old ones.

To those whose cooperation, interest, and enthusiasm have made possible this book, grateful acknowledgment is given. Among these are Dr. William G. Vinal, Professor of Nature Study, New York State College of Forestry, Syracuse University; Mr. Charles F. Smith, instructor in Scouting and Recreational Leadership, Teachers College, Columbia University; Dr. E. Lawrence Palmer, Professor of Rural Education, Cornell University; Mr. M. S. Koch, Jr., Boys Athletic League, New York, N. Y.; Mr. Garson Herman, M.A.; the Girl Guides who have been most generous in allowing us to use games from their books; and, of course, our own Girl Scout leaders and professional workers.

—Program Division
GIRL SCOUTS

CONTENTS

		PAGE
	INTRODUCTION	1
CHAPTER 1	MIXERS, ICE BREAKERS, AND STUNTS	3
CHAPTER 2	QUIZ AND MEMORY GAMES	17
CHAPTER 3	PAPER AND PENCIL GAMES	24
CHAPTER 4	ESPECIALLY FOR BROWNIES	29
CHAPTER 5	GAMES WITH BALLS, BEAN BAGS, AND ROPES	34
CHAPTER 6	RELAYS WITHOUT AND WITH EQUIPMENT	43
CHAPTER 7	NATURE GAMES	55
CHAPTER 8	CROSS-COUNTRY AND STALKING GAMES	83
CHAPTER 9	SAFETY-WISE GAMES	96
CHAPTER 10	WINTER OUTDOOR GAMES	99
	BOOKS FOR THE LEADER OF GAMES	103
	ALPHABETICAL INDEX OF GAMES	104

INTRODUCTION

GAMES FOR FUN and as a way of learning have always been important in the Girl Scout program. They play a vital role in the lives of young people, for they stimulate creativeness, initiative, and skill.

This collection is not classified by the Girl Scout program fields, although a few obvious ones, such as nature, out-of-doors, and Safety-Wise games, have been used. Games for other fields may easily be adapted; for example, making a relay game of setting tables or making up charades for the dramatic field. One must remember, however, that games are not always the best way to learn or practice certain activities, such as first aid, for instance.

Each game has been designated as suitable for different age levels to facilitate selection. A game designated for Brownies may be suitable for Girl Scouts of Intermediate age, and those for girls of the Intermediate age may be enjoyed by older girls. As a matter of fact, many of the games included, presented with slight variation, may be used for a leaders' meeting or by Senior Girl Scouts planning a program for parents and friends.

A bibliography of additional helpful material and an alphabetical index are given at the end.

How to Select and Present a Game

In selecting a game the purpose should be kept well in mind. A leader may be planning an afternoon of sheer relaxation, an outdoor meeting, a party, or she may be looking for a few games to use during the regular troop meeting. A game wisely selected may be found useful in putting over special points in the program.

Game time may be a torture to the shy child or a bore to the know-it-all. Obviously a great deal depends on the ability of the leader to solve these problems. She will soon learn that a shy child will be better placed where she can win easily, and the bored or dictatorial players may be asked to keep score or referee.

In presenting a game the leader must know the rules, formation, and general procedure. She must also be able to give directions clearly and concisely. There will then be no hesitancy or uncertainty on the part of the players and they will not lose interest. A few basic hints may help to assure a happy time:

1. The Girl Scouts themselves should be permitted to share in the selection of games. Taking charge wherever possible gives them excellent practice and increases their self-confidence.

2. Consider equipment and space available. Low lights and windows in a meeting place, for instance, offer serious obstacles in ball games.

3. Prepare ample material. It is better to have too much than not enough

4. Demonstrate the game whenever possible before playing.

5. In choosing up sides change the method from time to time. Play games by patrols, by teams formed by counting off (the group electing a captain). or by selecting captains to choose their own teams.

6. When a number of games are to be played, schedule the ones using the same kind of formation in succession, especially with large groups. Thus, circle games follow circle games; games with teams in files follow each other; and so forth.

7. Alternate quiet games with active ones.

8. Begin with a simple game or one already known to the group; build the game program to a climax so that you can finish with a game that is sure to make a hit.

9. See that everyone is occupied and interested.

10. Have the group under control at all times. Use an agreed-upon signal. such as raising the hand for attention, instead of a whistle.

11. Take an active interest either as player, referee, or audience.

12. Stop the game before it "dies." Tactfully change to another game.

13. Make sure everyone understands when the game is won. Girls should be encouraged to play for the sake of the game and their side, and to applaud the winning team. In competitive games it is necessary to recognize the winners.

CHAPTER 1

MIXERS, ICE BREAKERS, AND STUNTS

MIXERS AND ICE BREAKERS

Getting Acquainted
Intermediate and Senior

SPACE: Meeting place or large room.
FORMATION: A circle with a player in the center.
PROCEDURE: Each girl must know the names of the girls on either side of her. Give two minutes to learn the names of these new friends. The girl in the center of the circle points to someone and says, "left" or "right." The girl pointed to must give the name of the neighbor indicated before the girl in the center counts ten. If she cannot, she changes places with the girl in the center of the circle.

VARIATION I: After the game has been played as above, the leader blows a whistle six or seven times. The group forms circles of that number and the girls are then asked to give the names of their neighbors to left or right. Repeat several times.

VARIATION II: Girls take partners and march in a double circle. At the sound of the whistle, the inside circle about faces and marches in the opposite direction. At the sound of the second whistle, the girls take new partners and talk a minute to exchange names. Repeat several times.

Animal Team Race
Brownie and Intermediate

SPACE: Large room or out-of-doors.
FORMATION: Players in teams of equal number, arranged in file formation.
PROCEDURE: Girls in each file are given the names of animals: for instance, the first, rabbit; the second, elephant; the third, kangaroo; and so on down the line. Upon a signal from the leader the first girl of each file goes to a certain point about twenty feet beyond the starting line and back again imitating the movements of the animal she has been named. She then touches off number two who goes in her particular manner and so on until all have played.
FINISH: The line first finishing wins the game.
Points might be given for the best imitations, instead of speed.

Farmyard

Brownie

SPACE: Large room or out-of-doors.
FORMATION: Teams in files.
PROCEDURE: Each file chooses the name of an animal that is easy and amusing to imitate, then all are blindfolded and scatter about the room. At a signal the animals start making their own noises to attract other members of their own tribe. For instance, the "ducks" start quacking as they wander around the room. If they hear other quacks they make for that direction. When two ducks meet, they take hands and seek other quackers. The first tribe to meet wins the game. This is great fun but terribly noisy.

Buddy Game

Intermediate and Senior

SPACE: Meeting place.
PROCEDURE: Each girl chooses a partner she has not before known. They learn five things about each other so that each can introduce her buddy to the group instead of introducing herself. Among the five things to learn about a buddy might be: Where is she from? What is her Girl Scout rank and her interest in Girl Scouting? Why is she at your meeting? What is her favorite food and magazine? What is her hobby? What color are her eyes?

Torn Pictures

Intermediate and Senior

SPACE: Meeting place or out-of-doors.
EQUIPMENT: A sheet of paper for each Girl Scout. A quarter sheet of newspaper will do very well.
PROCEDURE: After dividing the group into several equal teams and numbering them, each player holds the piece of paper behind her and tears out of it the following:
Ones, a Red Cross emblem; twos, an American Flag; threes, a Girl Scout in uniform; fours, a robin; fives, a daisy; sixes, a maple leaf; sevens, a life preserver; eights, an open book.
About two minutes are given for this, after which the members of each team in turn hold up their efforts and the troop votes on the best. The team having the largest number of votes wins. Have the girls suggest good emblems to tear out.

MIXERS, ICE BREAKERS, AND STUNTS

Buzz
Intermediate and Senior

SPACE: Meeting place.
FORMATION: Players sit in a circle.
PROCEDURE: Players start counting in turn and at any multiple of five or seven—five, ten, fifteen, fourteen, twenty-one, or any number ending in seven (twenty-seven, thirty-seven)—the player must say "buzz" instead of the number. When a player says "buzz" in the wrong place or says a number where she should have said "buzz" she pays a forfeit. The girls who have not paid forfeits win the game.

Skip, Run, or Sit
Brownie and Intermediate

SPACE: Meeting place or outdoor playground.
FORMATION: One person in the center of a double circle.
PROCEDURE: Skip or walk around the circle in opposite directions. Leader says "change," and circle turns and goes in opposite direction. When the leader blows whistle or claps hands everyone must take her original partner and sit on the floor with hands joined. This may also be accompanied by music and when the music stops the players must sit on floor with their partners, hands joined.

Newspaper Costumes
Intermediate and Senior

SPACE: Meeting place.
EQUIPMENT: Four sheets of newspaper and twelve pins to each girl for half of the players.
PROCEDURE: Within a given time, half of the girls of each team are dressed by their teammates with the newspaper and pins. Points should be given to teams for speed and effectiveness.
VARIATION: Make hats only. (Clever hats can also be made by using paper plates, paper cups, and napkins.)

Crosses
Brownie, Intermediate, and Senior

NOTE: This game is a variation of musical chairs.
SPACE: Large room or out-of-doors.
GROUND MARKS: A number of crosses are drawn on the floor down the center of the room, or on the ground, one fewer than there are players.

PROCEDURE: The players stand around the crosses all facing counter clockwise. They start going around them obeying the leader's orders, such as, "hop," "run backwards," "walk." At the word "sit" each player runs for one of the crosses and sits down on it. One player will be left out. After each round, one cross is erased and the game continues until all the players but one are out.

Bumps
Brownie, Intermediate, and Senior

SPACE: Large room.
EQUIPMENT: One chair for each player.
FORMATION: Chairs in a circle.
PROCEDURE: The one who is "it" leaves her chair vacant and stands in the center of the circle. Immediately the player sitting to the left of the vacant chair moves into it, the next player moves into the chair just vacated, and the entire circle of players continues to move rapidly, clockwise, around the circle, while the one in the center tries to seat herself in a vacant chair. When she succeeds, the player to her left becomes "it."

Out of Squares Jerusalem
Intermediate and Senior

SPACE: Large room.
EQUIPMENT: Bean bags or small objects, such as horse chestnuts.
FORMATION: Players in a large single circle.
GROUND MARKS: Draw five small squares on the floor within the players' ring.
PROCEDURE: The objects used are placed in the squares, one fewer than the number of players. At a signal, the players march forward around the circle to music. When the music stops, each player tries to secure an object. The player left without one is out of the game. One object is then removed and the game continues.

Bird's Nest
Brownie, Intermediate, and Senior

SPACE: Meeting place.
FORMATION: Players sit in chairs in a circle.
PROCEDURE: One player is "it" and sits in the center. The girls decide upon three or four birds that they know and each girl takes one of the birds' names decided upon. The player in the center calls one of these names and

tries to find a place as all of the birds of that name change places. This leaves another player in the center who becomes "it" and continues by calling the name of a bird. When she calls "Bird's Nest" all the players change places.

Balloon Battle
Brownie and Intermediate

SPACE: Large room.
EQUIPMENT: Two or three balloons.
FORMATION: Players in two teams. Each team stands in two ranks, one behind the other, facing the opposing team, and with about two feet of space between the ranks and teams. Players may sit or stand.
PROCEDURE: The leader tosses up two or three balloons between the teams and they bat the balloons, each trying to make them go over the heads of the opposing team.
FINISH: One point is scored for the team batting the balloon over the opposite team. It a balloon goes out at either end it does not score, but is tossed in again by the leader and the game continues.

Holes
Brownie and Intermediate

SPACE: Meeting place.
EQUIPMENT: A large sheet of wrapping paper or newspaper for each team.
PROCEDURE: Pieces of various shapes and sizes are cut from each sheet of paper and scattered around the room. Each team is then given the paper with the holes in it and at a signal everyone except the team captain tries to find the pieces of paper that will fit the holes in her team paper. The team captain remains in the corner with the large sheet and tries to fit the pieces brought in. Any pieces that she finds do not belong in her sheet of paper should be taken back and dropped where they were found.
FINISH: The team that first fills its sheet correctly wins.

Milady Goes to Paris
Intermediate and Senior

SPACE: Meeting place.
FORMATION: Players sit in a circle.
PROCEDURE: The leader says "Milady went to Paris and bought a fan," and she imitates the movement of using a fan. This is repeated all around the circle until everyone has said the words and is waving a fan. The leader then says, "Milady went to Paris and bought a fan and a pair of scissors,"

and imitates the movement of using scissors with her other hand. Milady continues her shopping, purchasing articles that bring into play first the right then the left foot of each player. Next she catches a cold and keeps saying, "Ker-choo." Last of all, she dies (lies flat on the floor).

This game may be varied by adding any other motions the girls can think of to do.

Images
Brownie, Intermediate, and Senior

NOTE: In Japan, images of Buddha occur in five hundred different poses: hands raised above head, hands holding sides, hands on thighs, playing a trumpet, and so on. From these poses the Japanese have made the following game, which is played by old and young alike.

PROCEDURE: Any number of players stand in a circle and each strikes a different pose. They then recite the following rhyme:

"Rakansan, rakansan, rakansan ga,
Sorottara-soro soro
Hajime ya janaika
Yorija, so no so
Yorija, so no so."

At the repetition of the last line everyone changes her pose to that of the player on her right. Then the rhyme is repeated again and at the last line poses are again changed. No pose may be taken by two persons at one time, and anyone who fails to take the pose of her neighbor drops out of the circle.

If the Japanese rhyme is too unfamiliar to use, almost any familiar nursery rhyme will serve the purpose just as well and the pose may be changed on the last word of the rhyme. Better still, let the players make up a rhyme of their own for this game.

Drummer Man
Brownie, Intermediate, and Senior

SPACE: Meeting place.
FORMATION: The players sit in a semicircle.
EQUIPMENT: Imaginary musical instruments for each player.
PROCEDURE: The drummer man is the orchestra conductor. All hum some well known tune and imitate the actions necessary for the playing of the instruments. When all are playing the drummer man changes his instrument for another in the orchestra. The member whose instrument he has taken must at once play the drum; the drummer man then takes a third

instrument and the owner must immediately take the one that the drummer man was playing, and so on. Whenever the drummer man reverts to his drum, all must at once play their own original instruments.

Eliza Crossing the Ice
Brownie, Intermediate, and Senior

SPACE: Meeting place
FORMATION: Teams in files.
EQUIPMENT: Each team has two sheets of newspaper folded in four.
PROCEDURE: This game is played as a relay. The folded papers are cakes of ice and at the word "go," each number one—or one and two may start together if there is room—puts one piece down in front of her and steps on it with one foot, puts the other piece down a little ahead and steps on that. Then she reaches back for the first piece of paper while balanced on the forward foot, puts that piece in front of her and swings her free foot forward to it. She keeps repeating the process until she has gone around a given object and back to touch off the next person in her team. The first team finished wins. If a girl puts her foot down on the floor (into the river) she is out (drowned) unless her team throws her a bowline and saves her so that she may begin over again. She cannot shuffle along on the two papers but must reach back, get the paper, and step forward each time.

Gossip
Intermediate and Senior

SPACE: Meeting place.
FORMATION: Players sit in a circle.
PROCEDURE: The leader begins the game by whispering a sentence to the player on her right. The second person repeats it to the third exactly as she hears it and so on around the circle back to the leader. The sentence must never be repeated twice; the players must listen carefully.
FINISH: The sentence that returns has never been known to be the same as the one that started!

Rabbits in a Trap
Brownie and Intermediate

SPACE: Large room or out-of-doors.
FORMATION: Eight players form a fairly large double circle and then two by two make arches, which are the traps.
PROCEDURE: The rest of the players—the rabbits—run around the circle through the arches. At a signal they may be caught if they are under the

arches. Those who are caught form more arches, and the rest of the rabbits go on running through until they are caught.

Ring Game
Brownie, Intermediate, and Senior

FORMATION: Group sits in a circle on chairs. "It" is in the center.

EQUIPMENT: Rope or string with a ring on it, long enough to go around the circle.

PROCEDURE: Each player has her hands on the rope, and the ring is passed around the circle. "It" tries to locate the ring, but the players all keep their hands moving to hide its position. The girl who holds the ring when "it" finds it must be "it" the next time.

Tag Games
Brownie and Intermediate

These tag games are tried and true and should be played out-of-doors as far as possible.

Hang Tag

Players must hang on to something, with both feet off the ground to avoid being tagged. Positions must be continually changed.

Singing Tag

Leader announces a song to be sung. "It" tries to tag someone before she finishes singing the song.

Double Tag

Each player has a partner with whom she must clasp hands. The game is played like ordinary tag. Any couple tagged becomes "it."

Collar Tag

"It" tries to put a Girl Scout tie around the neck of another. A player may not raise her hands above her waist to prevent "it" from trying to put the tie on her.

Partner Tag

One player volunteers as runner and one as chaser. The rest take partners, hook arms, and scatter over the playing area. The runner tries to hook the arm of any person, thus setting an original partner free. If the chaser catches the runner before she hooks on to another person, the situation is reversed.

If the runner is successful in hooking on to someone, the other partner must then become the runner.

Back-to-Back Tag

SPACE: Large room or out-of-doors.

PROCEDURE: A player is chosen to be "it" and can tag anyone who is not standing back to back with another player. No one may stand by the same person longer than five seconds.

Spin the Platter

Brownie, Intermediate, and Senior

SPACE: Meeting place.
EQUIPMENT: Pie pan.
FORMATION: Players, numbered, form a circle.

PROCEDURE: One player starts the game by spinning the platter in the center of the circle, calling out a number as she does so. The player with that number must catch the platter before it has stopped spinning. She sets it spinning again and calls out another number. Thus the platter should be kept spinning the whole time by one or another of the players.

FINISH: Anyone who fails to catch the platter before it falls loses one of her three "lives." Three failures and she must drop out.

Yes or No

Intermediate

SPACE: Meeting place.
EQUIPMENT: Beans or peanuts.

PROCEDURE: This game may be used from the time the first players arrive at the meeting until all are present. The leader gives each player ten beans upon her arrival. The girls proceed to ask each other questions pertaining to some Girl Scout work studied, trying to get "yes" or "no" for a reply. If any girl answers a question by either word she must forfeit one bean to the inquirer.

FINISH: At the end of the game, the girl having the largest number of beans wins the game.

Automobile Race

Intermediate and Senior

SPACE: Large room or out-of-doors.
FORMATION: Teams are lined up in file.

GROUND MARKS: Starting line; finishing line about twenty feet beyond.
PROCEDURE: Each player is given the name of an automobile and told what is wrong with it.
FOR EXAMPLE: All the number one players—Ford—right tire flat (players hop on one foot). All the number two players—Chevrolet—can only use reverse (run backwards). All the number three players—Packard—all right (players run on all fours) and so on for each player in the file. When the leader calls out the name of one of the cars, those with that name run to a given point and back doing their particular stunt.
FINISH: The first one back to her place scores one point for her team.

Foreign Shopping
Intermediate and Senior

SPACE: Meeting place.
FORMATION: Groups of four or five sitting in various parts of the room.
PROCEDURE: One player from each group comes to the leader. The leader gives them an order (all have same one) to be bought in a foreign store where they cannot speak the language. These players return to their groups and act out the orders. The lips must not form the words, but each word must be *acted*. Use words that can be easily acted; often words with more than one meaning are fun to do.
EXAMPLES: Two hot dogs with onions; three cold turkey sandwiches; one pound of spaghetti; four feet of blue lace; and so forth.
This game is an excellent introduction to dramatics.
FINISH: The first group to guess the order is the winner. Another actor is chosen from each group and new orders are given by the leader, and so on until several girls have had an opportunity to act.

STUNTS

Stunts may be used by all age groups with equal enjoyment. In this group, taken by permission from a collection, *Individual Stunts without Equipment* by Garson Herman,* hundreds of variations can be made that are interesting and stimulating. Care should be taken not to overdo the more strenuous of these activities. Such simple stunts as these may be fun in themselves and in addition afford practice in balance and coordination for sports, folk dancing, and so forth.

Balance Kick

Brownie, Intermediate, and Senior

OBJECT: To do a balance kick.

DESCRIPTION: Start in a slight knee-bend position. Hop sideward left, as far as possible, on the right foot and at the same time kick the left leg sideward to the left. Land on the right foot, with the body in an erect position.

HINTS:
1. Use the arms for balance and lift.
2. Practice long hops to the left side.
3. Practice kicking the right leg to the right side without shifting the body to the right side.
4. Keep the eyes focused straight ahead.

VARIATIONS:
1. Repeat the stunt hopping sideward right.
2. Repeat the stunt alternating left and right to rhythm.

Blind Man Squat

Brownie, Intermediate, and Senior

OBJECT: To do a full squat with the eyes closed or blindfolded, without shifting the feet.

DESCRIPTION: Start in a standing position, feet slightly separated, eyes blindfolded. Bend the knees slowly and at the same time raise the heels. Bend the knees as far as possible. Return to the original position.

HINTS:
1. Keep the back straight throughout the bending.
2. Use the arms for maintaining balance.
3. Use the toes for balance.

---

*Copyrighted 1939 by Garson Herman, B.S., M.A., 106 Great Kills Road, Great Kills, Staten Island, New York.

VARIATIONS:
1. Repeat this stunt with the hands on hips.
2. Repeat with the hands grasped behind the back.
3. Repeat with the arms folded in front of the chest.

Bullet Spin

Brownie, Intermediate, and Senior

OBJECT: To spin in the air.

DESCRIPTION: Start in a standing position. Bend the knees slightly and spring into the air, spinning completely around, returning to the original position.

HINTS:
1. Spring as high as possible.
2. Use the arms for height and spin.
3. Keep the body erect.

VARIATIONS:
1. Repeat trying to make two or more complete spins.
2. Repeat with the eyes closed.
3. Repeat with the arms folded across the chest.
4. Repeat with hands clasped behind the head.
5. Repeat with the hands on the hips.

Camel Strut

Brownie, Intermediate, and Senior

OBJECT: To imitate the walk of a camel.

DESCRIPTION: Start in a standing position with the feet well apart. Bend the body forward touching the hands on the floor, in front of the feet. Spread the arms apart. Walk forward, in this position, to a designated spot.

HINTS:
1. The elbows and knees should be locked (arms and legs stiff).
2. The weight should rest on the hands.
3. The right hand and the right leg should move together, alternating left and right.
4. Keep the head high.

Double Heel Click

Brownie, Intermediate, and Senior

OBJECT: To jump into the air and kick the heels together twice, landing with feet apart.

DESCRIPTION: Starting in a standing position, bend the knees slightly, then spring into the air clicking the heels twice at the height of the spring. Spread the feet apart while landing.

HINTS:
1. Swing the arms upward and sideward to reach maximum height.
2. Land on toes for balance.
3. On landing, bend the knees slightly to prevent jarring the body.

Double Russian Side Step
Brownie, Intermediate, and Senior

OBJECT: To do a step of a Russian folk dance.

DESCRIPTION: Start in a full squat position. Place the left hand on the floor outside of the left foot. Extend both legs sideward. Return to the original position. Repeat ten times rhythmically.

HINTS:
1. Keep the elbows stiff.
2. Rest the weight of the body on the left hand.
3. Use the right arm for balance and spring.

VARIATIONS:
1. Repeat the same stunt, placing the right hand on the floor.
2. Alternate left and right.
3. This stunt may be made difficult by placing the hand on the hip.
4. It may be made more difficult by placing the hand behind the head.

Duck Strut
Brownie, Intermediate, and Senior

OBJECT: To imitate the walk of a duck.

DESCRIPTION: Start in a standing position, the feet about twelve inches apart. Do a full squat. Place the arms between the legs, grasping the heels with the hands. In this position walk forward, taking short steps.

HINTS:
1. Keep the body as erect as possible.
2. At each step lean the body sideward to imitate the waddle movement of a duck.
3. Move the head up and down, but keep the eyes focused straight ahead.

VARIATIONS:
1. This stunt may be made difficult by walking backward.
2. It may be made more difficult by walking sideward.

Squat Spring

Brownie, Intermediate, and Senior

OBJECT: To spring into an erect position and return.

DESCRIPTION: Start in a deep knee-bend position. Keep the trunk erect and spring into the air, straightening the knees, and return to a deep knee-bend position. Repeat ten times.

HINTS:
1. Use the arms for balance and height.
2. Jump as high as possible—the higher the jump, the easier the stunt.
3. Keep the body straight, the head up.

VARIATIONS:
1. Repeat this stunt with the eyes closed.
2. Repeat with the hands folded in front of the chest.
3. To make this stunt difficult, repeat with the hands clasped behind the back.

CHAPTER 2

QUIZ AND MEMORY GAMES

INCLUDED HERE are the question-and-answer type of games and sense-training games through observation and memory. They may be adapted to any subject in which the troop as a whole is especially interested. If all the girls like to sing they may enjoy a tune-guessing game. Another form of quiz game made popular by the radio is that of identifying a well known person through a series of facts about him. The girls will probably enjoy it more if each team supplies the questions (and answers) for the other; this would have to be done the week before, however, so that the leader could edit the questions and check the answers.

This form of activity may be used in all the ten fields of interest of the Girl Scout program.

Washington Crosses the Delaware

Intermediate and Senior

NOTE: This is a good way to review Girl Scout program activities.
SPACE: Large room or out-of-doors.
FORMATION: Two teams face each other with a wide space—the Delaware—between.
PROCEDURE: Each side has a George Washington who stands just in front of the line. Questions are asked on alternate sides down the line. A correct answer entitles George to one step forward, and an incorrect answer passes the question to the other side.
FINISH: The George who crosses the Delaware first wins for her team.

Number Relay

Intermediate and Senior

SPACE: Large room or out-of-doors.
FORMATION: Teams in files facing their team captain, who stands fifteen or twenty feet away.
PROCEDURE: The leader asks a question, the answer to which is a number. For instance, "How many stars in the Big Dipper?" or other appropriate questions.

Each team answers the question by having the correct number of girls to indicate the answer run around the team leader and return to the end of their team file. As soon as the required number runs forward, the rest of the team steps up to the starting line in order to keep all members in the line ready for action.

Points may be given to teams in accordance with the speed and accuracy of their answers.

Citizenship Game

Intermediate and Senior

SPACE: Meeting place.

EQUIPMENT: A black house in the center of the room and a white house in each team corner, and an envelope full of questions or statements on citizenship and community problems for each patrol or team.

FORMATION: Each team is in a corner; on a chair, half way between it and the center of the room, is an envelope containing the team questions.

PROCEDURE: A girl in each team runs to her team's chair and gets one slip from the envelope. If the statement or question on it is one that she can answer in the affirmative, she takes the slip back to her white house; if the statement is incorrect she takes the slip to the black house in the center of the room.

FINISH: When all slips have been taken, each white house is visited by the leader who checks the slips and discusses the questions with the whole group. The team who has the highest score of correct answers wins.

Twenty-One Questions

Intermediate and Senior

SPACE: Meeting place.

PROCEDURE: One player leaves the room. The others decide on something that she must guess by asking questions that can be answered by yes or no. She is allowed twenty-one questions to guess. Suppose the group has decided upon the Bastille. The player returns and asks, "Is it in the 'animal kingdom'?" "No." "Is it in this country?" "No."—and so on from one person to the next in order until she guesses or has had twenty-one questions.

Indian Guessing Game

Intermediate and Senior

SPACE: Meeting place.

FORMATION: The group sits in a circle.

PROCEDURE: A person chosen to be "it" leaves the room. A member of the group is chosen to start making motions and when "it" returns she tries

QUIZ AND MEMORY GAMES

to guess which player started the various motions that the members of the group are making.

She is given two guesses. Change "it" each time, as well as the person who leads the motions.

Listening
Intermediate and Senior

SPACE: Indoors or out-of-doors.
EQUIPMENT: Pencils and paper for each player.
FORMATION: The group sits in a circle facing outward.
PROCEDURE: The leader makes a series of noises. When she has finished the players write them down in order. Then the girls change papers and the leader reads out the right list while the girls make corrections. At least twelve sounds should be given.

VARIATION: Two or three girls act a scene inside the circle. The rest of the group guess by sounds what takes place. The girl with the best account of the action wins.

Actions
Intermediate and Senior

SPACE: Large room.
EQUIPMENT: Pencils and paper.
PROCEDURE: The group, divided into several small teams, watches the leader who performs twelve actions rapidly, one after the other. Then all teams run around the room three times, after which they take their notebooks and pencils and write down in order all the actions remembered. Their lists are checked by the leader to see which team has the best score.

Girl Scout Baseball
Intermediate and Senior

SPACE: Gymnasium floor or out-of-doors.
NUMBER OF PLAYERS: Two teams of nine each.
EQUIPMENT: A set of numbered questions written on separate slips of paper and a set of correct answers for the umpire.
GROUND MARKS: Four bases and a pitcher's box.
PROCEDURE: The game is played like baseball except that instead of throwing a ball, the pitcher draws a question from a hat and "throws" it to the Girl Scout at the bat. If the batter is unable to answer, she may ask the pitcher the same question. If the pitcher is unable to answer correctly, the batter

takes her base on balls. (No strikes allowed.) If the batter answers correctly, she runs to first base. If she does not know the correct answer and the pitcher does, the batter is out. If the second batter answers correctly, the first batter runs to second base. The leader should perhaps act as umpire. After a question is "thrown," the umpire counts ten. Any member of the opposing team may "catch" the ball by answering, after the batter has had her chance. Three "outs" retire the side. Score as in baseball—one run for each player to reach home.

Quicksight

Intermediate and Senior

SPACE: Indoors.
NUMBER OF PLAYERS: *Small group.*
EQUIPMENT: About twenty articles placed on a table.
PROCEDURE: Each player in turn is allowed to look for thirty seconds at the objects on the table, then she must turn her back while they are removed. She has two minutes in which to replace them in their original positions.

NOTE: This game may be played with a pack of cards and may be carried on simultaneously in different parts of the room.

Camp Equipment

Intermediate and Senior

SPACE: Meeting place.
FORMATION: Players sit in a circle.
PROCEDURE: One player begins, "I went to camp and took with me a _____," naming some part of her equipment. The next player must repeat that sentence and add to it an additional item that she took. As the game continues each player must repeat the whole sentence as it accumulates, and then add something new. When each player has had a chance to play, the one that started says, "When I got home from camp I unpacked my_____," and mentions all the items but her own, which was the first of all. The next player mentions all but her own addition and so on until there is only one item left for the first player to mention.

Guaranteed to induce concentration!

Look Sharp

Brownie, Intermediate, and Senior

SPACE: Meeting place.
FORMATION: Teams stand in two lines facing each other.

QUIZ AND MEMORY GAMES

PROCEDURE: Each player has a partner on the opposite team. The players are given one minute in which to observe their partners carefully. On signal, they turn back to back and each changes three items of her attire. For instance, she may undo a button, untie a shoe lace, and alter the position of her Girl Scout pin. At the next signal all turn face to face again and each observes the changes in her partner's attire.

FINISH: Team captains count up the score of their teams. Each change noted counts one point.

Feeling
Brownie, Intermediate, and Senior

SPACE: Indoors.

EQUIPMENT: A dozen or more small articles and paper and pencil for each player.

FORMATION: Players sit in a circle blindfolded.

PROCEDURE: The leader passes a series of small articles around the circle for the players to handle and pass slowly from one to another. No one article may be retained for long. The girls then make a list of what they have felt. Examples of things to be passed: velvet, chamois, leather, thimble, hairpin, bean bag, feather, fur, and blotting paper.

Pictures
Brownie, Intermediate, and Senior

SPACE: Meeting place.

EQUIPMENT: A picture of a well known person, building, or place cut out of a newspaper without its title and brought to the meeting by each Girl Scout.

PROCEDURE: The pictures are numbered and passed around to be correctly named.

FINISH: The patrol or team whose members identify the largest number of pictures wins.

Authors
Intermediate and Senior

SPACE: Meeting place.

EQUIPMENT: A set of cards on which are written names of well known authors, and another set on which are written titles of four of their books, one to each card.

PROCEDURE: Each team captain is given the name of a different author. She sends out one girl at a time to find the name of a book written by that author. The names of the books are scattered around the room. When the team has found the four books, they take another author and try to find his books.

FINISH: The team completing two sets first wins.

There are many variations of this game, using signaling, flowers, birds, trees.

Look-See

Brownie, Intermediate, and Senior

SPACE: Meeting place.

EQUIPMENT: About fifteen small objects.

PROCEDURE: Pass around fifteen small objects, such as a spool of cotton, pen point, key, library card. The leader then asks twelve or fifteen questions about these things, such as, what is the number of the spool of cotton, when does the library card expire, what make is the pen point. Make some difficult points of observation, such as a pin prick on a postage stamp.

FINISH: The team who has the largest number of correct answers wins.

Finger Sight

Brownie, Intermediate, and Senior

SPACE: Meeting place.

EQUIPMENT: Several different kinds of fruits or vegetables about the same size, such as pear, peach, apple, orange, tomato.

FORMATION: Two teams sitting in two parallel lines.

PROCEDURE: Blindfold the captain of each team and every other person in the line, or half of each team, and pass the fruits or vegetables to them. Each blindfolded player has an assistant who writes down the names of the fruit or vegetable as they are given to her by the blindfolded player.

FINISH: The team with the largest number of correct answers wins.

Dumb Crambo

Intermediate and Senior

SPACE: Meeting place.

FORMATION: Players sit in a circle.

PROCEDURE: One player goes out while the rest decide what animal she is to represent. Then she comes back and stands in the circle and tries to find out what animal she is supposed to represent. She asks each player in turn a question that can only be answered by "yes" or "no."

"Have I four feet?" "Yes."

"Have I long ears?" "No."
"Have I sharp teeth?" "Yes."
"Do I live in North America?" "Yes."
"Am I rare in North America?" "Yes."
"Do I swim?" "Yes."

The one in the center asks a question of each player until she has guessed correctly. Then the last person questioned takes her place.

Dom Dom — A Variation of Dumb Crambo
Intermediate and Senior

The group may be divided into two sides: One side to answer the questions, and one side, which has privately selected an animal, or bird, or flower, to give the questions to be answered. Questions must be answered correctly by "yes" or "no" and when the answer has been found, the sides change off.

Nope
Intermediate and Senior

SPACE: Meeting place.

EQUIPMENT: Several objects placed in a row.

PROCEDURE: A player goes away while the group selects an object. When she returns her partner points to one that was not selected, asking, "Is it this?" The player replies, "Nope." His partner continues to point to the wrong objects until the reply is "No" instead of "Nope." This is the signal that the right object should now be pointed out. Accordingly the partner points to it, asking some question as before, and the player declares it to be the right one. In repetition of this game a variation may be made by reversing the use of "nope" and "no" so as to baffle any players who may think they have guessed the system.

Remembering Shapes
Senior

SPACE: Meeting place.

EQUIPMENT: Paper and pencil for each player.

PROCEDURE: The leader exhibits a paper with geometric shapes or similar objects to the group and then asks the girls to draw as many as they remember.

CHAPTER 3

PAPER AND PENCIL GAMES

PAPER AND PENCIL GAMES appear throughout this collection. The ones that follow do not logically fit under other headings and have therefore been placed in a separate group. They are mental gymnastics excellent for quiet play, small meeting space, and adult groups.

Crazy Groceries
Intermediate and Senior

SPACE: Meeting place.

EQUIPMENT: A pencil and paper for each girl.

FORMATION: Players are divided into two equal teams. Each team sits in a circle.

PROCEDURE: Each girl writes down the name of an article sold by a grocer with the letters jumbled. Upon a signal each girl passes her slip to her right-hand neighbor, who tries to decipher it correctly. At each signal the slips are passed on whether they have been deciphered or not. Points are scored for the team whose members soonest decipher their slips.

VARIATION: Instead of putting the name of an article sold by the grocer on the slip, Girl Scouts might write down the names of articles to go into a first aid kit or articles of personal or troop equipment or equipment to take on an overnight hike.

Tourist
Senior

SPACE: Meeting place.

EQUIPMENT: Paper and pencil for each player.

PROCEDURE: Each player is asked to plan a tour that will take her from her home town on a complete tour of the United States. She may travel either east or west, north or south, but before her return she must have visited every state in the Union. By writing names of states one after another, each player indicates her route. To win, the player must not only complete her list first, from memory, but must have chosen a route that does not jump over states. It is surprising how many will try to go from Minnesota directly to Montana or from Texas into Mississippi.

NOTE: It is well to have a map of the United States on hand to settle disputes. To make this game a real "stickler," try Canadian provinces.

Words from Words

Brownie, Intermediate, and Senior

SPACE: Meeting place.
EQUIPMENT: A pencil and paper for each girl.
PROCEDURE: A word of ten letters or more is chosen, such as "denominator" or "antiseptic." The players are to make words of not fewer than four letters using the letters of the chosen word. If the word "denominator" is taken, for example, such words as "demon" and "mentor" could be made.

FINISH: At the end of a prescribed time, one point may be given for every correct word of at least four letters and two points for each word that no other player has.

Ty's

Intermediate and Senior

SPACE: Meeting place.
EQUIPMENT: Paper and pencil for each player.
PROCEDURE:

1. The best policy   (*honesty*)
2. Forever and ever   (*eternity*)
3. First and always   (*safety*)
4. Brotherhood   (*fraternity*)
5. The spice of life   (*variety*)
6. What killed the cat   (*curiosity*)
7. Pleasing to the eye   (*beauty*)
8. Where we all live   (*community*)
9. What we have been enjoying   (*levity*)
10. Heat, power, and light   (*utility*)

FINISH: The person finishing first or the one completing the greatest number of blanks at the end of a specified time wins.

Shop Window Race
(For City Girl Scouts)

Intermediate

SPACE: A business block.
EQUIPMENT: Pencils and paper.
PROCEDURE: The leader, who acts as umpire, takes a group, divided into teams, past three shop windows, giving the players thirty seconds to stop at each. She then takes them a short distance away, provides them each with

pencil and paper and asks them to write from memory what they noticed in two of the three windows.

FINISH: The girl who writes down the greatest number of articles correctly scores for her team.

VARIATION: Have the girls walk past a block of business houses and then ask them where certain things can be purchased.

Penny Game

Senior

SPACE: Meeting place.

EQUIPMENT: A penny and paper and pencil for each player.

PROCEDURE: Give a Lincoln penny to each of the players. Have them look at it a couple of minutes and then collect the pennies. Then give each player a copy of the following list of things found on a penny.

1. Name of a snake................................(*copperhead*)
2. A messenger ....(*one cent*)
3. A country ....(*U. S. A.*)
4. A fruit..(*date*)
5. An animal ....(*hair — hare*)
6. A building ....(*temple*)
7. Top of a hill..................................(*brow*)
8. Part of a river...............................(*mouth*)
9. Ourselves ....(*we*)

FINISH: The person finishing first or the one completing the greatest number of blanks at the end of a given time wins.

Arithmetic Game

Intermediate and Senior

SPACE: Meeting place.

EQUIPMENT: Paper and pencil.

PROCEDURE: Read the following to players:

Take your age two times
Add 5
Multiply by 50
Add any amount of change under $1
Subtract 365 days in one year
Add 115 for good measure

ANSWER: The two left-hand digits give you your age and the two right-hand ones equal the amount of change you added.

What Letter?

Intermediate and Senior

SPACE: Meeting place.
EQUIPMENT: Paper and pencil for each player.
PROCEDURE: Fill in the blanks with single letters of the alphabet.

Human organ .... (i)
Beverage .... (t)
Vegetable .... (p)
Bird .... (j)
Insect .... (b)
Clue .... (q)
Part of the house .... (l)
Large body of water .... (c)
Sheep .... (u)
Command to oxen .... (g)
Exclamation .... (o)

FINISH: The person who finishes first or has the greatest number of blanks completed at the end of a specified time wins.

Flower Game

Intermediate and Senior

SPACE: Meeting place.
EQUIPMENT: Paper and pencil for each player.
PROCEDURE: Fill in the blanks with names of flowers.

Kitten .... (*Morning glory*)
Sunrise .... (*Tulips*)
A kiss .... (*Four o'clock*)
Middle of the afternoon .... (*Jack in the pulpit*)
Preacher .... (*Dandelion*)
King of beasts .... (*Phlox*)
Crowd of sheep .... (*Star of Bethlehem*)
Christmas Eve .... (*Bachelor's button*)
Unmarried man .... (*Flags*)
Star-Spangled Banner .... (*Pansies*)
Your thoughts .... (*Poppy*)
A girl's father .... (*Lady's slipper*)
Worn on girl's foot .... (*Golden rod*)
Gilded cane .... (*Scarlet sage*)
Wise man with a red face .... (*Pussy Willow*)

A bird in old clothes...............................(*Dogwood*)
Queen of the flowers.............................(*Ragged Robin*)
Plant a puppy and what would
  come up ....(*Rose*)

FINISH: The person who finishes first or has the greatest number of blanks completed at the end of a specified time wins.

CHAPTER 4

ESPECIALLY FOR BROWNIES

THE GAMES in this section are suitable for Brownies and younger Girl Scouts.

Magic Music

SPACE: Meeting place.
FORMATION: Players sit in a circle or in an informal group. One player is "it" and leaves the room.
PROCEDURE: The players decide on something in the room that "it" must touch. "It" returns to the room and, as she walks around trying various objects, the players sing some pre-arranged song. As "it" gets "warm," the players sing loudly; as "it" gets "cold" they sing softly. They try to show by shades of loudness and softness just how warm "it" is.

When the group becomes experienced, the game may be made more complicated by having "it" do something (close the window, sit on a chair, and so forth) instead of just touching an object.

When the game is first introduced, it may be made easier if the leader claps her hands or taps on a tin cup, and so forth, instead of having the children sing. Then she will be sure they understand the game.

Find a Seat

SPACE: Meeting place.
FORMATION: Players sit on chairs in a circle. One player is "it."
PROCEDURE: "It" strolls around the circle motioning to various other players to follow. The group skips around the circle until "it" claps her hands. Then all scatter to find seats. The player without a seat is "it" and starts the game over.

Touch and Follow

SPACE: Meeting place.
FORMATION: Players sit in a circle.
PROCEDURE: The first player touches an object in the room. The second player touches that object and another one. The third player touches those two and adds another, and so forth. This continues round and round to see who can remember the most objects. This game is good for a small group.

Thread the Needle

SPACE: Meeting place.

FORMATION: Players are divided into two large teams. Teams line up facing each other with members of each team holding hands.

PROCEDURE: Each team counts off beginning with one so that each player has a number corresponding to a number on the other team. The leader calls two consecutive numbers and on each team the players with those numbers raise their hands that are joined to form an arch. For example, if six and seven are called, the players with those numbers on each team form an arch. On each team the end players lead their lines through the arch and back to place. Both ends go at once, and the ends must go first. Players must not drop hands. The team first back in place in a straight line wins. The play continues until one team has a specified number of points.

Brownies and Fairies

SPACE: Large room or out-of-doors.

FORMATION: Players are divided into two teams of equal number and form two parallel lines twenty to forty feet apart. One group is called Fairies, and the other Brownies.

PROCEDURE: The Fairies turn their backs to the Brownies. The Brownies then move slowly and quietly toward the Fairies. When quite near the leader calls out, "Look out, the Brownies are coming!" and instantly the Fairies turn around and chase the Brownies back to their starting line, trying to tag as many as possible. If a Brownie is tagged, she joins the Fairies. This is repeated with the Brownies doing the chasing.

The team that has the greatest number of players at the end of a definite time is the winner.

Brownie Chariot Race

SPACE: Large room, or outdoor playground.

FORMATION: Players are divided into groups of three—two horses and one driver.

EQUIPMENT: Rope or colored streamers for reins.

PROCEDURE: The horses join their inside hands, making a team. Each horse holds one end of the rope in her outside hand and the driver holds the other ends. The teams line up at a starting line. At the signal "go," they race to the finishing line. The finishing line may be twenty-five or thirty yards straight ahead or in a circle. The team that finishes first wins.

Frog in the Sea

SPACE: Large room or outdoor playground.

FORMATION: Players form a circle around five "frogs" who sit with their feet crossed, tailor fashion.

PROCEDURE: The players in the circle dance or skip close to the frogs and back, repeating the words, "frog in the sea, can't catch me." The frogs try to tag any player, without rising or uncrossing their feet. If a frog succeeds in tagging a player she changes places with her and the tagged player becomes a frog. Or, the player who is tagged may sit in the circle with the frogs instead of changing places. The game continues until there is one player left to be tagged.

In dramatizing this game, the frogs' place may be a sea, pond, brook, creek, or river and the players in the circle may represent snakes, grasshoppers, or animals who move in characteristic fashion.

Hawk and Doves

SPACE: Large room or out-of-doors.

FORMATION: Players are divided into two teams—the doves. Each flock of doves has a "dove cote" marked on the floor or ground about ten yards apart. One player is chosen as the hawk and stands half way between the cotes.

PROCEDURE: The hawk claps her hands to frighten the doves and they all come out of their cotes, either one at a time or all together, and try to get into the other cote. If touched by the hawk, a dove is put into a cage at one side and must remain there until the next dove is caught, who takes her place. Thus there is only one player in the cage at a time. If the doves do not come out of the dove cote when the hawk flaps her wings, she may catch them in their cote.

Midnight (Twelve o'Clock at Night)

SPACE: Large room or outdoor playground.

FORMATION: Two goals are indicated, several yards apart—the fox's den and the chicken yard. One player is the fox, another the mother hen, and the rest are the little chickens.

PROCEDURE: The mother hen arranges her chickens in a compact group and then leads them up close to the fox's den and inquires, "If you please, Mr. Fox, what time is it?" If he replies any hour except midnight they are safe and may play about. The hen allows them to play a moment and then gets them together again. Standing between them and the fox the mother hen again asks the time. If he replies, "Twelve o'clock at night," they must run to the chicken yard. Anyone caught is taken to the fox's den. The last remaining chicken becomes the fox and the game is played over again.

Come Along

SPACE: Large playing area.

FORMATION: Players stand in a single circle facing the center, with left hands extended in front of them.

PROCEDURE: A player who is chosen for starter runs around the inside of the circle, grasps hold of someone's left hand with her right, swings her into the center of the circle, and takes her place. The player in the center then grasps the hand of another, and so on until the whistle blows, then all rush back to their original places. The last player in place stands in the middle of the circle and chooses someone to start the play again.

Old Hen and Chickens

SPACE: Large room or outdoor playground.

PROCEDURE: Choose a player to be the old hen who leaves the group. All others sit with their heads bowed. The leader touches four players on the head. Immediately they become little chickens. The old hen is recalled and when she says, "Cluck, cluck" the four wee chicks answer, "peep, peep." The mother hen tries to locate them by sound.

The chick discovered first becomes the old hen. The object of the game is to try to keep the mother hen from guessing which chick is answering.

Eenie, Weenie, Coxie, Wanie

SPACE: Large room or out-of-doors.

FORMATION: Group scattered over the playing space.

PROCEDURE: The one who is "it" clasps her hands in front of her and says "Eenie, Weenie, Coxie, Wanie," and proceeds to tag someone with her clasped hands. The one who is tagged becomes her partner. These two players join hands, and the new girl repeats the words, "Eenie, and so on" and the pair proceeds to tag someone with their clasped hands. The next person tagged clasps hands with the first two. The newly tagged person must stand still and repeat the above words so all can hear her before another person may be tagged.

The game continues until only one player is left who has not been tagged. This person becomes "it" for the next round.

Fish and Net

SPACE: Large room or out-of-doors.

FORMATION: Half the players form a line at one end of the playing area with hands joined to represent the net. At the other end are the fish.

PROCEDURE: At a signal from the leader, all the fish try to run to the opposite end of the playing space without being caught in the net. The net must try to encircle as many fish as possible. Those caught become a part of the net. Only the girls at the ends of the net may use their hands to catch the fish. The rest of the net tries merely to encircle the fish. If the net breaks all the fish may escape.

When all the fish have been caught, the players change roles.

Jingling

SPACE: Large room or roped-off area out-of-doors.

EQUIPMENT: A bell.

PROCEDURE: All of the players but one are blindfolded. This player has her hands tied behind her and a bell tied around her neck. The blindfolded players try to catch the jingler and she tries to confuse them. Any girl who strays out of the roped-off area removes her blindfold and remains out of the game until the jingler is caught.

CHAPTER 5

GAMES WITH BALLS, BEAN BAGS, AND ROPES
GAMES WITH BALLS

Tower Football
Intermediate

SPACE: Large room or out-of-doors.
EQUIPMENT: Three wands or long sticks, one basket ball or volley ball.
FORMATION: Players in a single circle with one person in the center.
PROCEDURE: The player within the circle defends the tower, which is formed by three wands or sticks tied together and placed in the center. The players forming the ring kick the ball toward the center, trying to knock the tower down. The player who succeeds in knocking the tower down with the ball becomes the defender of the tower.

Corner Ball
Intermediate and Senior

SPACE: Large room or out-of-doors.
EQUIPMENT: Volley ball or basket ball.
GROUND MARKS: The space is divided in two by means of a chalk line, and a small square goal is marked off in each of the four corners.
PROCEDURE: The players divide into two teams, which occupy opposite courts with a goal-keeper in each of the two goals on the opponent's side. The other members of the team may not cross the center line nor enter their opponents' goals. The leader tosses the ball up between two opposing players in the center of the field and the members of each team try to get the ball and throw it over the heads of the opposing team to either of their own goal-keepers. If a goal-keeper catches the ball while standing within her goal, she scores a point for her team, otherwise the ball goes to the other side for a free throw. A goal-keeper having scored a point throws the ball to one of her own side, over the head of her opponents, and the game continues.

Twenty points make a good game.

Team Passing
Intermediate and Senior

SPACE: Large room or out-of-doors.
EQUIPMENT: One basket ball or volley ball.

FORMATION: Two teams, distinguished by arm or head bands, are placed about the room in couples (opponents).

PROCEDURE: The ball is tossed up by the leader between any two opponents. The player who secures it passes it at once to another of her own side who quickly passes it again and so on. The aim of the game is to secure as many consecutive passes as possible. The game is greatly improved by having every six consecutive catches score a goal, resulting in a new start from center. This prevents the scoring from becoming erratic. The leader keeps the score by calling out the number of passes as they are made. Neither capturing the ball at the start nor intercepting a pass scores a point. Players may not hold the ball for more than three seconds. If two hold the ball, the leader tosses it up between them and a new "break" is started.

This is good preparation for various team games and can be elaborated and improved upon by any group.

Indoor Rounders
Intermediate and Senior

SPACE: Large room

EQUIPMENT: Basket ball or volley ball.

FORMATION: One team in a file, the first girl being at the bat; the members of the other team are scattered about the room to act as fielders.

PROCEDURE: The leader throws the ball to the girl at bat, who bats it with her hand as far as possible and immediately begins running around her own file. The fielding team retrieves the ball as quickly as possible, and each fielder falls in behind the girl who has caught the ball. She passes it back over the heads of each one. When it reaches the last girl, she calls "stop!" The girl who batted must stop running around her file immediately and take up her place at the back of the line, while the next girl goes up to bat. Each batter keeps count of the number of times she completely circles her file, and after every member of the team has batted, the total runs are added up and the fielding team has its turn at the bat.

Spud
Intermediate and Senior

SPACE: Large room or out-of-doors.

EQUIPMENT: Volley ball or large rubber ball.

FORMATION: Players in a single circle.

PROCEDURE: One player stands in the center of the circle, tosses the ball up, and calls the name of one of the other players. All but the one called scatter immediately, lest they be tagged by the ball. The player called catches the ball and tries to hit one of the other players with it. She may not run, but must throw from where she secures the ball. If she misses, she retakes the ball, stands where she recovers it, and tries again, the other players fleeing before her as before. If she hits a player, that one immediately secures the ball and tries to hit someone else with it. The second one hit tries to hit a third one and so on.

Whenever a player misses hitting another with the ball, it is called a "spud" and counts one against her; three spuds put the player out.

Ball Puss
Brownie and Intermediate

SPACE: Large room or out-of-doors.
EQUIPMENT: Any soft ball.
PROCEDURE: This game is much like "Puss-in-the-Corner." Walls or parts of a building or trees may be used for corners, or corners may be marked on the ground. One player is "it," and the others occupy the corners. Players change places and "it" tries to hit one of them with the ball while they are changing. The one hit becomes "it."

If there are many playing, it is advisable to have several be "it."

Circle Stride Ball
Brownie and Intermediate

SPACE: Large room or out-of-doors.
EQUIPMENT: Basket ball or volley ball.
FORMATION: Players in a single circle facing the center.
PROCEDURE: Players stand with feet apart touching those of the next player. One is chosen to be "thrower" who stands in the center with the ball. She throws the ball, trying to get it through the circle. The others can prevent it only by using their hands. If the ball goes through the circle, the person whose feet it passed between or on whose right it passed then becomes the thrower.

Jumping Ball
Intermediate

SPACE: Large room or out-of-doors.
EQUIPMENT: One tennis or soft rubber ball for each team.
FORMATION: Teams line up in single file behind a starting point.
GROUND MARKS: Starting line and a goal line about twenty feet beyond.
PROCEDURE: The first player in each file is given a ball, which she places

between her feet. On signal, she tries to jump to the goal line and back, holding the ball firmly between her feet. She touches off the next in line, who repeats the play and so on until all have had a turn.

FINISH: The team that finishes first wins the game. Anyone who drops the ball must pick it up and go on without touching it with her hands.

Dodge Ball
Brownie, Intermediate, and Senior

SPACE: Large room or out-of-doors.

EQUIPMENT: Volley ball or large rubber ball.

FORMATION: Half the players form a single circle. The other half stand inside this circle.

GROUND MARKS: It is well to indicate by chalk marks the boundary of the circle.

PROCEDURE: The players in the circle have the ball, which they throw across the ring trying to hit one of the players inside. If one of these is hit below the knees she is "dead" and is out of the game. The inside players continue to try to avoid the ball until all are hit, then the two sides change places.

FINISH: The team whose players remain in the center longest wins the game.

Soccer Dodge Ball
Intermediate and Senior

SPACE: Large room or out-of-doors.

EQUIPMENT: Volley ball or large rubber ball.

FORMATION: Half the players form a single circle. The other half stand inside this circle.

PROCEDURE: The team on the outside keeps the ball in play by passing it with the foot or kicking it at the inside team, eliminating players as they are hit. The ball must be kept in play without touching ball with the hands. If the ball stops in the center of the circle, a player from the outside team must get it, using the feet to bring it back to place.

FINISH: The team that eliminates the greater number of players in a given time is the winner.

Squad Dodge Ball
Brownie and Intermediate

SPACE: Large room or out-of-doors.

EQUIPMENT: Volley ball or large rubber ball.

FORMATION: One team forms a single circle. The other team stands in the center of the circle in a single line, each player holding on to the waistline of the one in front of her.

GROUND MARKS: Mark the boundary of the circle.

PROCEDURE: The players in the outside circle have the ball and they aim to hit the end player of the center team with it. The team members in the center hold together and dodge about to avoid the ball. The outer circle continues the play, at no time holding the ball. Each team takes a turn in the center for two minutes. At the end of that time the team scores one point if its end player was not hit.

FINISH: The team holding the highest score at the end of the game wins.

Progressive Dodge Ball
Intermediate and Senior

SPACE: Large Room.

EQUIPMENT: Volley ball or large rubber ball.

GROUND MARKS: The playing space is divided up into three equal territories.

FORMATION: This is a game for three teams, each occupying one territory.

PROCEDURE: Begin with team A in one end space, team B in the center, and team C in the other end space. It is the aim of teams A and C to hit players of team B below the knees with the ball. Team B aims to hit players of either team A or C. Any one hit drops out. Team B players may not catch the ball after a straight throw from an opponent; one who does is out. They may pick up the ball after a bounce or rebound into their territory, then aim at a player on one of the other teams.

This continues until all of team B are out. Teams A and C then score as many points as there are players left standing on their sides.

Team A then goes to the center territory and when all its members are out, teams B and C count their scores. Then team C goes to the center area and the game is repeated.

FINISH: At the end of the three rounds the team having the highest total score wins the game.

Circle
Brownie, Intermediate, and Senior

SPACE: Large room or out-of-doors.

EQUIPMENT: Two balls or bean bags for each side.

FORMATION: Single circle; alternate players are on the same side.

PROCEDURE: Two girls, standing side by side, have their balls in front of

BALLS, BEAN BAGS, AND ROPES 39

them. At a signal, each girl picks up her ball and passes it around the circle to each player on her own team.

FINISH: The first team to pass the ball around the circle five times wins.

Hit the Bat
Intermediate and Senior

SPACE: Large room or out-of-doors.
EQUIPMENT: Bat and soft ball.
FORMATION: Two teams as in baseball.
PROCEDURE: When the batter hits the ball she must lay the bat down across home plate and run the bases, without stopping. Whoever fields the ball must roll the ball back to home plate and try to hit the bat before the runner returns home. If she is successful the runner is out. If she isn't, the runner scores a point for her side. The runner is also out if the ball, when batted, is caught in the air. Three strikes put her out. Three outs for a side constitute an inning.

GAMES WITH BEAN BAGS

Overtake Pass
Brownie and Intermediate

SPACE: Out-of-doors or meeting place.
EQUIPMENT: Two bean bags of different colors.
FORMATION: Sixteen to twenty players in a single circle, facing center, numbered off by twos.
PROCEDURE: A number one on one side of the circle, and a number two on the opposite side are each given bean bags. On signal, both pass the bean bags to their own players to the right. Each team aims to have its bean bag overtake that of the other.

Bean Bag Jerusalem
Brownie and Intermediate

SPACE: Large playing area.
EQUIPMENT: Bean bags or Indian clubs.
FORMATION: Teams in single file.
GROUND MARKS: Starting line and a goal line twenty to thirty feet beyond.
PROCEDURE: On the goal line are placed the bean bags, one fewer than there are files. On signal, the first player in each file runs and tries to secure

a bean bag. One will be unsuccessful. These players then go to the end of the line, the next ones in line repeat the play and so on until all have played.

FINISH: One point is given each team whose player gets a bag. The team having the highest total score at the end of a specified time wins the game.

Reds and Blues

Brownie and Intermediate

SPACE: Large room or out-of-doors.

EQUIPMENT: Twelve bean bags of two different colors.

FORMATION: Two teams. Half the members of each team stand in the enemy's territory, half in their own, the central space being neutral territory.

GROUND MARKS: Two lines across the playing space dividing it into three parts. The center may be smaller than the two end spaces.

PROCEDURE: Each team has six bean bags of the same color and on signal both teams start tossing them to their teammates over the way. The members of both teams try to intercept their opponents' bags. If an opponent's bag is caught it is put out of play.

FINISH: At the end of the game each team scores one point for each bag captured and two points for each one of its own that it has kept in play.

GAMES WITH ROPES

Sinking Ships—I

Intermediate and Senior

SPACE: Large room or out-of-doors.

FORMATION: Any number of teams of equal size. One girl acts as leader for each team.

EQUIPMENT: Fifteen feet of rope for each team.

GROUND MARKS: Two lines drawn across the playing area, about ten feet apart.

PROCEDURE: Team leaders, each holding a coiled rope, stand behind the line at one end of the playing space while the teams stand behind the line at the other. On the word "go" each team leader throws her rope to a member of her team, holding it by one end. The player who catches it ties a bowline around her waist before jumping overboard (over the line) and is then dragged across the room by the team leader. This "rescue" is repeated, the girl in each case tying and untying her own knot. If any knot is incorrectly tied, the girl "drowns."

FINISH: First team rescued wins.

Sinking Ships—II
Intermediate and Senior

SPACE: Meeting place.
EQUIPMENT: Newspapers and a length of rope.
PROCEDURE: The group is divided into two teams. Newspapers laid on the floor represent the ship. One team stands in line on the papers, the team leader is on shore facing them. The other team, divided into two groups one on each side of the ship, are waves. On signal, the waves rush forward and tear bits of paper with one hand and run back, while the team leader ties a bowline knot and throws it to a girl on the ship who puts it around her waist and is pulled to safety. The team leader then throws the rope to the next girl. Each girl of each team must be rescued in turn. While waiting to be rescued the members of the ship's crew try to prevent the waves from destroying the ship. The race is between the waves destroying the ship and the rescuer of the ship's crew.

Tie and Run
Intermediate and Senior

SPACE: Large room.
EQUIPMENT: One rope for each player.
FORMATION: Players in a single circle count off by twos to make two teams. One team should have an identifying mark.
PROCEDURE: A girl is chosen who steps outside of the circle, touches a member of the opposing team and calls out the name of a knot. They start around the circle in opposite directions, each tying the knot. Their aim is to tie the knot correctly and be the first to return to place.
FINISH: The one back first with the correct knot scores a point for her team. The other then touches a player of her opposing team and the procedure is repeated for a specified length of time, or until several kinds of knots have been tied.

Life Line Race
Intermediate and Senior

SPACE: Large room or out-of-doors.
EQUIPMENT: One rope for each girl.
FORMATION: Teams in files. One member of each sits on the floor facing her team about ten feet in front of it, and is the "victim."
PROCEDURE: Each girl holds a rope. The leader tells a yarn about a troop of Girl Scouts on a hike by a river. All at once screams are heard. A girl is

seen struggling beyond her depth in the water. What would the Girl Scouts do? Why, make a life line with whatever materials they can gather together. The teams have one minute to plan how they would make such a line. On signal each team makes a line by tying together their various ropes. They throw the line to the victim, who must catch it and be pulled to safety.

FINISH: The team that makes the first rescue using all correct knots wins.

Knot Relay

Intermediate and Senior

SPACE: Large room or out-of-doors.

EQUIPMENT: One piece of heavy twine or rope three or four feet long.

FORMATION: Four teams of six or eight each. Teams one and two stand in line, facing each other. Teams three and four also stand in line, facing each other.

PROCEDURE: One girl from each team, appointed to act as a post, takes her position facing in at each end of the passageway between the two facing teams. She holds her arms out straight in a horizontal position. On the word "go" the team leader of each line runs out and ties a reef or any other knot assigned on the nearest arm of the nearest post and runs back to place. She touches the hand of her next teammate, who runs out behind the line, takes the rope off the post, runs down between the ranks, ties the rope with the same knot to the nearest arm of the post at the other end, and comes back to place behind the line and touches the hand of number three. This is repeated to the last girl, who touches the hand of the team leader. She then holds up her hand and calls out the name of her team.

FINISH: The first team leader to call out the name of her team wins the game.

Knot Problem

Intermediate and Senior

SPACE: Meeting place.

FORMATION: Two or more teams.

EQUIPMENT: One rope for each player.

PROCEDURE: The leader states a problem, for example: "Your team has been asked to keep the crowd off a rather large area reserved for folk dancing at an outdoor playday. Each of you has a rope. What can you do about this request?" Each team leader gives the proper instructions to her team. The first team to form a guard-line correctly wins.

CHAPTER 6

RELAYS WITHOUT AND WITH EQUIPMENT

RELAY RACES can add a lot of fun to a meeting or a party. They can be adapted to almost any meeting place. It is wise to keep teams small, eight to ten in a team, so that the game will not drag or leave a large number of girls unoccupied at any given moment. They should be run off rapidly and not too many played at one time.

It is also wise to have a well marked or designated starting line behind which players must stand until they are tagged off.

The girls soon understand the drift of the game and then make up any number of additional relays. A number of interesting variations on the running relay may be planned according to the age level of players—hopping, jumping, skipping, or even going backward or sideways, instead of merely running.

Relays "with equipment" may include any paraphernalia available to indoor or outdoor groups, such as balls, bean bags, or other objects.

Brownies like relays in which they imitate animal actions, such as duck walk, rabbit hop, dog run, and so forth.

RELAYS WITHOUT EQUIPMENT

Run Around Relay
Brownie and Intermediate

SPACE: Meeting place.
FORMATION: Teams in files.
PROCEDURE: On signal the first person in each line runs around the right hand side of her team and up the left, continuing to a given goal in front of each file. She then returns and goes to the foot of her team, and immediately the next person does the same and so on, until all are back in their original places. Team finishing first wins.

Rescue Relay
Intermediate and Senior

SPACE: Meeting place.
FORMATION: Teams in files.
PROCEDURE: The leader of each team stands at a goal, a certain distance from her team. On signal the leader runs forward and takes the hand of the first person of her team and takes her back to the goal. The person taken to

the goal must then return for the next person, and so on until all are rescued. Players must not break clasped hands, if they do they are fouled and must run their turn over. The team that first gets all its players to the goal wins.

Centipedes
Intermediate

SPACE: Lawn, sand, or gymnasium mats indoors.

FORMATION: Players are divided into teams of equal number. A team kneels in file formation, each member holding on to the ankles of the person in front of her to make a centipede.

PROCEDURE: On signal the files begin to move forward, keeping step. If a centipede breaks it must go back and start again.

FINISH: The centipede that reaches a given point first wins the race.

Running Relay
Brownie, Intermediate, and Senior

SPACE: Meeting place or out-of-doors.

FORMATION: Teams in files.

PROCEDURE: On signal the first girl in every file runs to a goal (a wall or other designated spot) and returns, tags off the next in line, and goes to the end of the line. Each girl runs up and back when she is tagged until all have had a chance. The first team to finish wins.

VARIATIONS: Run up, walk back.
Skip up, skip back.
Walk backwards both ways.
Walk sideways both ways.

Shuttle Relay
Brownie and Intermediate

SPACE: Meeting place or out-of-doors.

FORMATION: Players form teams, which are divided in two parts that stand facing each other.

PROCEDURE: On signal the first player of file number one runs the distance between the two lines of her teammates. She then goes to the end of file number two, tags the first player, and takes her place in line. This player then runs up and down between the two lines and tags the second player in the first file, and so on, with players shuttling back and forth until each has run the distance once and stands in the line opposite to the one in which she started.

FINISH: The team that first makes a complete change of all players wins.

Backwards Relay
Brownie, Intermediate, and Senior
SPACE: Large room.
FORMATION: Teams in files behind a starting line.
GROUND MARKS: Starting line; finishing line about twenty feet beyond.
PROCEDURE: The game is a race run backwards on all fours. The players in each file get into position, heels on the starting line and backs to the finishing line. On signal the first players in each file all start going backwards on all fours.
FINISH: The first one to the finish line scores a point for her team. Then the next in line repeats the play. When all the players have finished the team having the most points wins.

Partner Relay
Brownie, Intermediate, and Senior
SPACE: Large room.
FORMATION: Players stand in double files, partners lock elbows.
GROUND MARKS: Starting line and a goal line about thirty feet beyond.
PROCEDURE: On signal the couples at the head of each file begin walking fast toward the goal line, inner elbows hooked together. Each time the leader blows the whistle the couples stop and make a complete turn and then go on. The leader may give such signals as often as she likes. Upon return the first couple touches off the second couple and it repeats the play, and so on.
FINISH: The file finishing first wins the game.
VARIATION: Have players in threes, with one walking backward.

Balance Relay
Intermediate and Senior
SPACE: Large room or out-of-doors.
EQUIPMENT: A small block of wood for each team.
FORMATION: Teams in files.
GROUND MARKS: Starting line and a goal line about fifteen feet beyond.
PROCEDURE: The first player in each file is given the piece of wood, and on signal she places it on her head or balances a stone on it and walks to the goal line and back balancing the object. If it falls off she must return to the starting line and try again. She returns, touches off the next in line who repeats the play, and so on.
FINISH: The file that finishes first wins the game.
VARIATION: Let each player ring a bell or whirl a whistle on a string while balancing the wood on her head.

Salute Relay

Intermediate

SPACE: Meeting place.
FORMATION: Teams line up in files, the team captains about ten paces in advance, each captain facing a team not her own.
PROCEDURE: At a given signal, the first player in each line runs to the team captain facing her and gives the Girl Scout salute smartly. If the salute is given with good form, the team captain returns the salute. If it is poorly done, the team captain does not return the salute, and the player must continue saluting until her salute is returned. Then she runs to the back of her own file.
FINISH: The file that finishes first wins a point.

Chalk Line Relay

Brownie and Intermediate

SPACE: Large room or out-of-doors.
FORMATION: Teams in files.
PROCEDURE: A line is drawn on the floor or scratched in the earth about thirty to forty feet in front of each team. The players walk the chalk line. If a player steps off the line she must recover her balance and continue at the point where she lost it. When she returns she tags off the next person who does the same thing and so on until all her teammates have had a chance.
FINISH: The team that finishes first wins.

Siamese Relay

Intermediate and Senior

SPACE: Meeting place.
FORMATION: Teams in files.
PROCEDURE: Each team divides into couples. The couples stand back to back, with bodies bent forward and hands clasped between their legs. In that position they run to a specific point and back without turning. The next couple does the same, and so forth.
FINISH: The team that finishes first wins.
VARIATIONS: There are many interesting and enjoyable variations to this relay. The following are examples of what can be done:
1. Same starting position as original relay. The couples run sideward (side stepping) instead of forward and backward. This variation is really a stunt. It requires closer cooperation and rhythmical movements.

2. Partners stand back to back and lock elbows. In this position they run to a designated spot and back without turning.

RELAYS WITH EQUIPMENT

Newspaper Race
Intermediate and Senior

SPACE: Meeting place.
FORMATION: Teams in files.
EQUIPMENT: Newspapers or cardboard.
PROCEDURE: The first player receives two sheets of newspaper. She walks to a designated place on the floor, stepping only on the papers; after each step the paper must be removed forward. She then runs back to line, handing the paper to the next player who does the same, and so forth.
FINISH: The team that finishes first wins.

Obstacle Relay
Intermediate and Senior

SPACE: Meeting place.
FORMATION: Teams in files.
EQUIPMENT: Chairs, benches, mats, apparatus, and so forth are placed around the playing space.
PROCEDURE: The first player in each file walks around, under, or through the various objects and back to her place. She touches off the second player who does the same, and so forth.
FINISH: The team that finishes first wins.

Circle Change Relay
Intermediate and Senior

SPACE: Large room or out-of-doors.
EQUIPMENT: Small objects, such as balls, rocks, sticks, and so forth.
FORMATION: Teams in files.
PROCEDURE: Draw two circles in front of each team. Place an object in one of each pair of circles. On signal the first person in line runs forward and changes the object from one circle to the other and comes back to tag off the next person, and then goes to the end of the line. The next person then runs forward and changes the object back again, and so on, until all have had a chance to change the objects. The team that finishes first wins.
VARIATION: Two or more objects may be used in each circle. Players should take care, however, to put objects inside of circle line.

Pass and Around Relay

Brownie, Intermediate, and Senior

SPACE: Large room or out-of-doors.
EQUIPMENT: One ball or bean bag for each team.
FORMATION: Teams in files.
PROCEDURE: The leader at the head of each file has a ball or some other object to pass. On signal the leader passes the ball to the person in back of her to the right side, and each person after that does the same in turn all the way down the line. When the end person gets the ball, she then passes it back to the leader to the left side. When the leader again receives it, she runs with the ball to a given point and returns, handing the ball to the next person in line, and goes herself to the end of the line. The second player then proceeds in the same way, and so on.
FINISH: The first team to return to its original position wins.

In and Out Relay

Brownie, Intermediate, and Senior

SPACE: Meeting place.
FORMATION: Teams in files.
EQUIPMENT: Three chairs for each team.
PROCEDURE: Place three chairs in front of each team in a straight line. All the players of each team must run in file formation in and out of the chairs; touch an object or wall at a point beyond the chairs, and come back to the starting point the same way.
FINISH: The team that finishes first wins.

Limber Relay

Intermediate and Senior

SPACE: Large room or out-of-doors.
EQUIPMENT: One bean bag or other object for passing.
FORMATION: Teams in files.
PROCEDURE: The first player in each file holds the bean bag and on signal she commands "overhead" and the bean bag is passed along over the heads of the players. When the last girl receives it, she runs to the front of the file and commands "jump astride" and the bean bag passes down the line between the players' knees. The game continues until each player in the file has given a command. Other commands might be "left face," "face right and lift left knee."
FINISH: The team that finishes first wins.

GAMES WITH EQUIPMENT

Chair Sit Relay

Brownie, Intermediate, and Senior

SPACE: Meeting place.
EQUIPMENT: A chair for each team.
FORMATION: Teams in files facing a chair at the head of the file.
PROCEDURE: First person in line runs up to the chair, sits down on it and then returns to her place and tags off the next person, and then goes to the end of the line. The next person proceeds as the first and so on, until all have had a chance.
FINISH: The team that finishes first wins.
Interest may be increased by having the players take both feet off the ground as they sit in the chair.

Sit and Change Relay

Intermediate and Senior

SPACE: Meeting place.
EQUIPMENT: One ball or bean bag for each team.
FORMATION: Players sit in chairs, one in back of the other, in files.
PROCEDURE: On signal the first person in line passes the ball over her head to the next person, and so on down the line. When the last player receives it, she gets up and runs on the right hand side of her row and stands in front of the first chair. This is the signal for all the other members of her team to get up and sit in the chair in back of them. Then she sits down in the first chair and passes the ball back as before.
FINISH: The team that gets back to its original chairs wins.

Turn About Relay

Brownie and Intermediate

SPACE: Large room or out-of-doors.
EQUIPMENT: One ball or bean bag for each team.
FORMATION: Teams in files.
PROCEDURE: The first player in each file holds a bean bag. On signal she passes it over her head to the next player and so on down the line. As soon as it has passed a player's hands, she faces about in the opposite direction. When the last person receives the bean bag, she also turns around and starts the bag back again in the same manner.
FINISH: The leader who first holds the returned bean bag scores one point. Seven points make a good game.

Stoop and Stretch Relay

Brownie, Intermediate, and Senior

SPACE: Large room or out-of-doors.
EQUIPMENT: One ball or bean bag for each team.
FORMATION: Teams in files.
PROCEDURE: On signal the first person in each file drops the bean bag over her head onto the floor in back of her. The second person stoops and picks it up, tosses it over her head, and so on down the line. At the end of the line the last person runs to the front and the same is repeated until everyone is back to the original position.
FINISH: The team that gets back to its original places first wins.

Relay Ball Game

Brownie and Intermediate

SPACE: Large room or out-of-doors.
EQUIPMENT: One ball for each team.
FORMATION: Each team stands in file formation and its team leader sits facing it at the other end of the room with a ball in her lap.
PROCEDURE: On signal, the first girl runs to her team leader, picks up the ball, runs back and touches the wall at the opposite end of the room, and then goes back to her place in the file from where she throws the ball to the team leader and sits down. When the team leader has replaced the ball in her lap, the next girl repeats, and so on.
FINISH: The team that finishes first wins.

Over and Under Relay

Intermediate and Senior

SPACE: Large room.
EQUIPMENT: One basket ball and one marble or bean bag for each team.
FORMATION: Teams in files.
PROCEDURE: Each team leader is given a basket ball. On signal she starts the ball down the line by passing it over her head to the girl in back of her, who passes it between her legs to the girl in back of her, and so on alternately down the line. When the last girl in each line gets the ball, she runs to the head of the line and starts it down again. The team in which the leader reaches the head of the line first, scores. Play until a team wins two out of three, then play with marbles instead of basket balls.

GAMES WITH EQUIPMENT

Overhead Relay
Intermediate and Senior

SPACE: Large room or out-of-doors.
EQUIPMENT: One ball or bean bag for each team.
FORMATION: Teams in files.
PROCEDURE: The first player in each file holds a bean bag. On signal she tosses it back overhead to two, who tosses it to three and so on, until the last girl receives it. She then runs to the front and tosses it to the one behind her. The game continues thus until every girl has had a chance to be first in line.
FINISH: The team that finishes first wins.

Circle Pass Relay
Intermediate and Senior

SPACE: Meeting place or out-of-doors.
EQUIPMENT: Bean bags.
FORMATION: Players in a single circle facing center.
PROCEDURE: Players number off by twos, number ones forming one team, twos the other. The leaders of the teams stand together, each holding a bean bag. On signal, each begins passing the bean bag to the next player of her own team, ones passing to their right, twos to the left.
FINISH: The team that gets its bag to its leader first scores a point. The game is usually played until one team scores nine points.

Pass and Crawl Relay
Brownie and Intermediate

SPACE: Large room or out-of-doors.
EQUIPMENT: One ball or other object for each team.
FORMATION: Teams in files.
PROCEDURE: Each team passes the ball overhead until the last person gets it. She then crawls through the legs of her teammates to the head of the line, gets up, and runs forward to a given goal and comes back and passes the ball overhead again.
FINISH: The team that gets back to its original places first wins.

Zigzag Bean Bag Relay
Intermediate and Senior

SPACE: Meeting place or out-of-doors.
EQUIPMENT: One bean bag or ball for each team.

FORMATION: Each team is lined up in double line formation, lines facing each other. The members of a team count off, zigzag fashion.

PROCEDURE: Number one of each team has a bean bag. On signal she tosses the bag diagonally across to number two who tosses it back to number three and so on to the end of the line. As the last person gets the bag, she tosses it back to number one. The bag that reaches number one first scores one point for that team. Five points is usually a good number for a game.

Zigzag Circle Relay — A Variation

Brownie and Intermediate

EQUIPMENT: Five balls or bean bags for each team.

FORMATION: Each team forms two circles, one inside the other, and the players face each other.

PROCEDURE: Alternate girls in each circle on the same team play as above. The team that has all five balls back to the starter first, wins.

Jumping Rope Relay

Brownie and Intermediate

SPACE: Large room or out-of-doors.

EQUIPMENT: One jumping rope for each team.

FORMATION: Teams in files.

PROCEDURE: On a given signal the first person jumps rope forward to a given line or object, comes back and gives the rope to the next player in line and so on until all are back to their original positions. The team that finishes first wins.

Peanut Relay

Intermediate

SPACE: Meeting place.

FORMATION: Teams in files, either sitting or standing.

EQUIPMENT: Ten peanuts in shells for each team.

PROCEDURE: Players stand or sit, each holding the wrist of the person on her left with her left hand. Ten peanuts in shells are placed in front of the leader of each line. At a given signal using her right hand, the team leader picks up one peanut and passes it to the free right hand of her neighbor, then she picks up another and so on down the line. Each peanut must be passed down the entire line without any person releasing the wrist of the one on her left.

GAMES WITH EQUIPMENT

FINISH: The row that passes all the peanuts first, without breaking the wrist hold, wins.

Bouncing Ball Relay
Intermediate and Senior

SPACE: Large room or out-of-doors.
EQUIPMENT: One basket ball for each team.
FORMATION: Teams in files.
PROCEDURE: On signal the first person in line starts to bounce the ball, progressing to a designated goal, such as a chair, and continues bouncing the ball around the goal and back to the next person in line. The next person does the same and so on until everyone has had a turn. The first team to finish wins.

Raisin Relay
Brownie, Intermediate, and Senior

SPACE: Meeting place.
FORMATION: Teams in files.
EQUIPMENT: A saucer of raisins for each team, and a toothpick for each player.
PROCEDURE: The leader in each line has a saucer of raisins. On signal the leader spears three raisins on her toothpick and feeds them to the next person who eats them and takes the saucer. Each person in line continues until the last person has speared her three raisins.
FINISH: The team that finishes first wins.

Paper Bag Relay
Intermediate

SPACE: Meeting place.
FORMATION: Teams in files sitting on the floor.
EQUIPMENT: One large paper bag for each team.
PROCEDURE: The first person in line has a paper bag placed over her clasped hands. At a given signal she stands up, runs around her file to her original position and places the bag on the next person's hands, and then sits. Each person in line proceeds in this manner until everyone has had a chance to run.
FINISH: The team that finishes first and has the fewest number of tears in its paper bag wins.

Cowboy Relay

Intermediate and Senior

SPACE: Large room or out-of-doors.
EQUIPMENT: Girl Scout tie.
FORMATION: Teams in files.
PROCEDURE: The first person in line, on signal, runs up to a given goal and comes back and ties the tie with a specified knot on the next person in line. When finished she goes to the foot of the line; the person with the tie around her neck runs forward. This continues until all are back to their original places. The team that finishes first wins.

CHAPTER 7

NATURE GAMES

Roadside Cribbage
Brownie, Intermediate, and Senior

This game makes the miles roll by unnoticed on a hike and it can be played by either two or thirty-two girls.

PROCEDURE: The group decides what things are to be looked for: certain kinds of birds, flowers, trees, wild animals, snakes, rabbits, squirrels, bird or animal tracks.

Each player then gathers twenty-one pebbles, seeds, or nuts for counters. Whenever she sees any of the objects specified she calls "pegs," and throws away a counter. The girl who first "pegs" all of her counters wins. The team leader should see that during the game no one leaves the trail or road and that no one lags behind.

The game can be played on a city walk by "pegging" specified kinds of trees or shrubs or flowers, horses of certain colors, and dogs and cats. It may also be played by the seashore where boats, rare shells, leaping fish, crabs, or other sea animals or plants may be looked for.

Zoos
Brownie and Intermediate

SPACE: Meeting place.

FORMATION: Each team sits in a circle.

PROCEDURE: Captains of all the teams come to the leader who tells them the name of an animal, flower, bird, tree, or other object. The team captains then run back to their teams and draw the object named while their teammates observe. As soon as any girl thinks she knows what her team leader is drawing she runs to the leader and tells her. The first girl to tell correctly wins the game. Repeat the game, having another girl in each team do the drawing.

FINISH: Hold an exhibition of the drawings and discuss their weak points in observation.

Sounds
Brownie, Intermediate, and Senior

SPACE: Out-of-doors; may be played while hiking at night, while sitting around an evening campfire, or in the dark out-of-doors.

PROCEDURE: The teams or individuals, as the case may be, sit silently for ten minutes and at the end of that time each one recounts the noises she has heard and can identify. Sounds may be the rustle of wind in the leaves or pine needles, bird notes, crickets, frogs, the sound of water or of rain, and the noises made by movement of little animals among the twigs and leaves.

FINISH: The team whose members distinguish the greatest number of sounds correctly wins.

Pandora's Box

Intermediate and Senior

NOTE: Good for a small group.

EQUIPMENT: The leader gathers a variety of objects and hides them in a box or basket before the troop gathers. The objects may include: twigs, leaves, flowers, bits of bark, seeds, shells, lizards, snails, toads, insects, stones—anything from the environment that Girl Scouts should know.

PROCEDURE: The teams gather and fall in behind their team captains facing the leader. As she lifts an object out of the box and holds it before the team its name may be called aloud by anyone knowing it. The captains may keep score for their own teams or the leader may give the objects to the Girl Scout who names it first. In this case the score is kept automatically, since the team that holds the largest number of objects wins the game.

VARIATION: This game may be played with pictures of garden flowers, leaves, birds, animals, insects, and so forth.

Indoor Trail

Intermediate and Senior

A good rainy-day game.

SPACE: Large room.

EQUIPMENT: Paper and pencil for each girl. About twenty-five pictures of birds, flowers, insects, constellations, and animals, or specimens of rocks or other natural objects are placed around the room. Some may be placed so as to be seen easily, others in more difficult places. Twenty-five pictures or objects is a good number.

PROCEDURE: With their papers and pencils, the girls write down the name of every object they find. The team whose members find the greatest number and identify them correctly wins.

VARIATION: Drawings of different flowers, trees, insects, birds, animals, and constellations, with missing bills, tails, leaves, petals, wings, legs, stars, and so forth may be placed in different groups and the teams sketch these missing parts on their pads according to numbers. Incomplete statements about the objects may also be included.

Woodcraft Hike
Intermediate and Senior

NOTE: Good for use in winter.

SPACE: Large room.

EQUIPMENT: Pictures of birds and constellations and blueprints of leaves, plants, and twigs are placed around the room. Woodcraft signs should also be used and a real story may be prepared by bits of charred wood to resemble a deserted fire, tracks of animals, and so forth.

PROCEDURE: The leader explains that they are all to take a hike in the room. The teams then draw to see which one starts first. They set off at intervals, the team captains armed with pencils and paper. Each team is to make up a yarn about what they see and note the various plants, twigs, constellations, and birds passed on the way.

At the end of the hike teams are given a few minutes to write the story. The team captains read the stories out loud and the troop selects the best.

The Story by Tracks
Intermediate and Senior

SPACE: Meeting place or out-of-doors.

EQUIPMENT: Plaster casts of the tracks of a rabbit, dog, fox, weasel, and deer, and a trail that has been made in advance showing a story of what might happen to these animals. Thus the rabbit tracks may come from a thicket, further along a dog's tracks follow the rabbit; later fox tracks cross those of the rabbit. The rabbit is captured by a weasel and the fox is chased by the dog for a time but later he gives up this chase to follow a deer. Other variations of this story may be planned.

PROCEDURE: Teams follow this trail and each writes its version of what happened, with descriptions and habits of the animals whose tracks are found. Quail, squirrel, field mouse, and beaver's tracks may be marked along the trail.

Tree Facts
Brownie and Intermediate

SPACE: Meeting place.

EQUIPMENT: A cardboard leaf of a tree has been made for each team. Each leaf is cut into five jig-saw pieces with facts about the tree it belongs to on the back of each piece.

FORMATION: Teams in files; the pieces of all the leaves are placed about twenty feet away.

PROCEDURE: Each team is given the name of a different tree. On signal, the first girl in each file goes and selects a piece with a fact about her tree written on it. If she takes a wrong statement back to her team the girl next to her returns it and takes back a correct statement.

FINISH: The first team to complete its leaf wins.

VARIATION: This game may also be played with bird cards.

Secret Leaves
Intermediate and Senior

SPACE: Meeting place.

FORMATION: Teams sit or stand in small circles, each team numbered beginning with one.

PROCEDURE: On signal the number ones run up to the leader, who shows them secretly a leaf. When they have observed it sufficiently they run back to their teams and describe it as accurately as possible but do not name it. When each team has decided what the leaf is, the number twos run back to tell the leader. If a team can't come to a decision, number two goes to have a look at the leaf. For the next round, number threes look at a fresh leaf and so on.

FINISH: The team first to name a leaf correctly, scores. This game may be played by beginners and encourages accurate observation and description.

VARIATION: Pictures of birds may be used.

I Am a Tree
Intermediate and Senior

SPACE: Meeting place.

FORMATION: Teams sit in a circle or in two facing lines.

PROCEDURE: A member of one team starts the game by saying, "I am a tree and I have compound leaves." Since no one knows what tree it is with such little information she continues:

    2. My wood is hard.
    3. I taste rather bitter.
    4. My bark is very shaggy.
    5. I am native to North America.
    6. My fruit is nuts.
    7. I am a valuable timber.
    8. My name is of Indian origin.

ANSWER: I am a shag-bark hickory.

NATURE GAMES

Long before this, someone on the opposing team will no doubt have guessed the tree. A member of the other team then takes the floor and continues the game with, "I am a flower" or "I am a mammal," or star or whatever else she chooses to be.

FINISH: Only eight statements are allowed. The team whose member is describing a nature object counts a point for each statement she has to make as a clue. If the other team guesses the correct answer with the help of fewer than eight statements, it gets one point for every statement spared.

Two in One

Intermediate and Senior

SPACE: Large room or out-of-doors.

EQUIPMENT: Pencil and paper for each team and as many leaves from different trees as there are members in a team.

FORMATION: Teams in files, numbered from one up.

PROCEDURE: The leaves are placed on the floor or on a table several feet in front of the teams; a few feet away are paper and pencils for each team. On signal the number ones run up, look carefully at the first leaf, then draw it from memory as accurately as possible. On signal they return to their files and the number twos repeat the process, drawing the second leaf. This continues until every girl has drawn a leaf and named it.

FINISH: One point is awarded to the team that finishes first. Then the drawings are compared with the leaves and the girls choose the best likeness. One point is given to the team whose drawing is judged the best, and one point for every leaf correctly named.

Tree Identification Game

Intermediate and Senior

SPACE: Wooded place.

EQUIPMENT: Set of cards for each team with the name of a tree on each card.

PROCEDURE: Cards are placed in a pile a few feet ahead of each team. The number ones each pick up a card and find the tree it names, label it, and return to their teams. Then number twos go, and so forth.

FINISH: Leaders of teams check to see whether trees are correctly labeled. The team that labels the greatest number of trees correctly within the time limit wins.

VARIATION: Cards may be prepared for plants, ferns, mosses, and so forth, and the game may be played by having all of the girls start at one time.

Three in One

Intermediate

SPACE: Meeting place.

FORMATION: Players divide into two teams that stand in facing lines, about two feet apart.

PROCEDURE: Each team has a home base about five feet behind its line. In turn each team chooses an animal (or tree, bird, constellation), which it must act out by some stunt that will suggest the name. On the completion of the stunt, the other team confers and calls out its guess. If it is correct, the acting team must race to its home base while the guessing team attempts to capture its members before they reach safety. Any players tagged are made prisoners of the other team.

FINISH: Originality and effectiveness of the stunt, together with the number of prisoners, is taken into consideration when deciding on the winning team. Stress cleverness and imagination in stunts but do not forget the incentive of capturing prisoners.

Matching Leaves — I

Brownie, Intermediate, and Senior

SPACE: Out-of-doors or large room.

EQUIPMENT: A different kind of leaf, collected by the leader from the playing area for the number of players comprising a team.

FORMATION: Teams in files.

PROCEDURE: The leader numbers the leaves and displays them so all can see them. On signal number ones run off to match leaf number one. Upon the return of number one in a file, number two goes to match leaf number two, and so on until all leaves are matched. The file that finishes first wins the game.

At the end of the game discuss the trees from which the leaves were picked. This game may be played with any small object such as seeds, weeds, stones. Do not use specimens that should not be picked. Teach conservation.

Matching Leaves — II

Intermediate and Senior

SPACE: Out-of-doors.

PROCEDURE: The group divides into two teams and the leader carefully explains that everyone is to scatter and collect as many different kinds of leaves as she can, without taking two from the same tree or bush. At the end of three minutes, the leader signals the girls to return and they sit in a circle around her. Each player lays her leaves on the ground in front of her and the leader quickly examines them to see that there are no incomplete leaves or duplicates. The team whose members have the greatest variety of leaves wins a point. The girl who has the fewest leaves then holds up one leaf so that all may see it, and names it. If she is correct every player who has a leaf of the same kind must give it to her. If she is wrong, she forfeits her leaf to the player who corrects her and all the players with the same kind of leaf give it to the same person. The next player then picks up a leaf, names it, and is given all of the same kind of leaves if she names it correctly. This procedure is followed around the entire circle until every kind of leaf has been named.

FINISH: The team whose members have amassed the largest collection of leaves wins.

Leaf Hunt
Intermediate

SPACE: Out-of-doors or large room.

PROCEDURE: The group is divided into teams and each team is given a list of trees within a small radius of the playing space. At a signal from the leader, members of each team run to procure a leaf from the list.

FINISH: The first team with all of the leaves correctly brought in wins.

This can also be played by hiding blueprints of the leaves about a room.

Be sure that trees and shrubs are not harmed when leaves are taken from them.

Nature Puzzles
Intermediate and Senior

Puzzles may be made up by teams and used by way of competition around the campfire. Here are a few examples of such puzzles.

1. My first is in hockey, but not in baseball.
   My second is in voting, but not in recall.
   My third is in country, but not in town.
   My fourth is in kingdom, but not in crown.
   My fifth is in ocean, but not in sea.
   My sixth is in Paris, but not in Dundee.
   My seventh is in plenty, but never in lack.
   My whole is a tall tree, with nuts hard to crack!
   —Hickory

2. My cap is of the brightest red.

And in a stump I make my bed;
My coat is of the glossiest black
And a glint of green it does not lack;
My vest is clean, and white as snow;
I'm sure you've seen me nimbly go
About the trunk both high and low,
Drumming and tapping fast or slow,
Looking for insects I like to eat,
As I hold fast by my four-toed feet.

—Redheaded Woodpecker

Name the Leaves

Intermediate

SPACE: Meeting place.
FORMATION: Teams sit in files.
PROCEDURE: Pass a number of leaves down each file.
FINISH: The team that names the greatest number correctly wins.

VARIATION: Pile different kinds of leaves on the floor. The players are numbered and divided into two teams. The leader calls out the name of a leaf and the number of a player.

FINISH: Every player who picks out the right leaf scores a point for her team. The team with the most points wins.

Team Treasure Hunt

Intermediate and Senior

SPACE: Out-of-doors.
EQUIPMENT: A list of objects for teams to collect, given to each team leader. The list might include such things as pine cone, oak leaf, mullein leaf, pieces of limestone, and cocoons.
PROCEDURE: At a signal, the teams scatter and hunt for objects.
FINISH: The team that returns to the leader first with all the objects on the list wins the game. There is usually someone in the team who will teach the others. Have at least one object that is not too easy to find.

VARIATION: When the girls are on a hike, picnic, or meeting out-of-doors, have the teams hunt for as many kinds of flowers or leaves or ferns as possible within a given time, returning upon signal. If there are unidentified objects in any one team, see if any girl in another team can place them. If so, give her team one-half point.

FINISH: The team collecting and identifying the greatest number of objects wins the game.

Watching the Trail
Intermediate and Senior

This game is especially adapted for hikes in the country. It may be used with slight changes on a walk in the city.

PROCEDURE: The girls agree on a list of objects, such as birds, plants, flowers, or fungi that they are to look for on their hike, and the first girl who sees any one of the objects named scores for her team. Thus, if the object of a hike in early spring is to study flowers, the game might be scored depending upon difficulty in locating plants, as follows: trillium, two points; bloodroot, one point; hepatica, one point; bishop's cap, two points; wild ginger, two points; anemone, one point; wild currant, three points; lady's slipper, five points.

Nature Squares
Brownie, Intermediate, and Senior

SPACE: This is a quiet game suitable for troop meetings or for rainy day campfires.

EQUIPMENT: Pencils and paper marked off in the following manner for every player. Headings and letters in left hand column may be changed to suit the players or the circumstances.

	Flower	*Tree*	*Bird*	*Animal*	*Insect*
B					
S					
T					
M					
O					

PROCEDURE: At a signal the squares are to be filled in with the names of flowers, trees, birds, animals, and insects, the first name of which begins with the letter shown on the left hand.

Ten minutes are allowed to fill in the blanks. At the end of the time the leader calls for the names given. Scoring places a premium on unusual names, thus: if there are fifteen players and four give the same name, each individual scores eleven; if only one person has the name, fifteen is scored. Scores are kept by each person and the total score is given as the result. Or, names duplicated may be crossed out and the team with the greatest number of names left wins.

Subconscious Observation

Intermediate and Senior

SPACE: Meeting place.

EQUIPMENT: A display of ten or fifteen fruits, vegetables, flowers, rocks, and minerals.

PROCEDURE: Place the objects on a table in the center of the room. Do not call attention to them but about halfway through the meeting cover the table and have each patrol or group of girls list the fruits and so forth from memory.

Hexapod Questions

Intermediate and Senior

SPACE: Meeting place.

FORMATION: Two lines facing each other about ten feet apart.

PROCEDURE: Number one on one side calls out a question on insects and all who know the answer take a step forward. The correct answer is then called out. Number one on the second side calls next, then two on the first, and so on.

Sample questions:
What insect swims upside down?
What insects breathe through their "tails"?
What insects have hard top wing covers?
What adult insects never eat?
What insects lay their eggs on milkweed?

A step forward is taken each time the answer is known. Teams pass each other to opposing lines and then return to their original positions, which should require ten steps back and forth.

Hidden Quests

Intermediate and Senior

SPACE: Meeting place.

EQUIPMENT: Sets of small cards on which are written questions regarding minerals, metals, plants, stars, birds, and so forth. Team names are written on the backs of these and hidden around the room.

PROCEDURE: Each team must find its own set of cards and answer the questions.

FINISH: The team first to find and answer correctly all its set of cards wins.

Sample questions:

NATURE GAMES 65

What is the chemical sign for water?
What is the silver colored mineral used in thermometers?
What mineral is used in making china?
What minerals form brass?
What minerals form bronze?
What is the purest crystal form of carbon?
What rocks are best suited for building stones?
What are the main constituents of cement?
What does coal come from?

Star Pictures
Intermediate and Senior

SPACE: Meeting place.
EQUIPMENT: Fifteen paper stars for each team.
FORMATION: Teams in files.
PROCEDURE: The number one players in each file come forward to look at a diagram of a constellation shown them by the leader. They then return to their teams and place their paper stars to form the constellation shown them. The number twos correct any errors in the form of the constellation, run to the leader, and name the constellation. The leader or team leaders together may decide which constellation is best. The number threes then look at another constellation, and so on.

Place the Stars
Intermediate and Senior

SPACE: Meeting place.
EQUIPMENT: A dozen paper stars for each team.
PROCEDURE: Players in groups. The leader calls out the name of a constellation, such as Cassiopeia. Whereupon each team arranges its stars to picture the constellation mentioned.
FINISH: The first team to lay the paper stars correctly wins.

Rock Discoveries
Intermediate and Senior

NOTE: This game is for girls who are interested in rocks and minerals.
SPACE: Meeting place.
EQUIPMENT: Have the following articles in a central location for all teams, which are lined up like spokes of a wheel fifteen feet from the center: quartz, flint, chalk, copper wire, diamond, ruby, gold ring (these three from

the ten cent store!), pencil lead (graphite), talc, and electric light bulb.

PROCEDURE: Leader stands to one side and calls out questions. Number ones from each team run around their lines and try to be first in seizing the object necessary to answer the question. The girl who seized the correct object scores a point for her team. Number ones takes their places at the end of their files and number twos run next, and so on.

Sample questions:

What form of chalcedony was used by the Indians in starting fires?

What object is a form of rock originally made of the shells of small water animals?

What metal is used electrically because it is a good conductor?

What is the hardest mineral?

What precious stone is the second hardest mineral?

What metal was perhaps the first to be used by primitive man?

What mineral feels greasy and will not burn?

What is the softest mineral?

Other minerals and metals for which various questions will suggest themselves may be used.

Blotch
Brownie and Intermediate

SPACE: Meeting place.

EQUIPMENT: A box of crayons and an outline drawing of a bird or flower for each team leader.

PROCEDURE: The members of each team go one at a time and look at the original or a colored picture of the object outlined and report the location of the various colors. Without looking at the original, the leader follows their directions in coloring her outline. The finished pictures are then held up for the vote of the group.

FINISH: The team that has the best likeness of the object wins the game.

Birds of Prey
Intermediate

SPACE: A large room or level ground.

GROUND MARKS: Two chalk lines, one near each end of the playing space.

FORMATION: The group is divided into an equal number of teams, which stand in two lines facing each other. Each team represents two or more different birds. A girl who is a swift runner is chosen to be a bird of prey.

PROCEDURE: The leader or one of the players gives the call of the various birds that the teams represent. When the team members hear their call they must rush to get behind the other chalk line without being caught by the bird of prey. Birds may be caught when they are between the lines. The game continues until there is only one girl left. She becomes the bird of prey and the game is repeated.

NOTE: This game is more fun if there is someone in the troop who can imitate bird calls well. It is a good game and bird calling is lots of fun, so get busy.

Birds easily imitated are owls, flickers, chickadees, phoebes, red-winged blackbirds, oven birds, and crows.

Animal Notes
Brownie and Intermediate

SPACE: Meeting place.

PROCEDURE: Write the names of various animals on slips of paper and let each girl draw one. She must study the animal indicated by her slip. She should find out how it looks, its habits, home, food, how it cares for its young, and other interesting facts about it. At the next meeting she has two minutes to tell her patrol or team about her animal without naming it. Her teammates guess its name. They then vote on the best and most interesting description given and it is repeated to the assembled troop. Team descriptions in turn are voted upon by the troop and the winning team scores.

Who's Who in the Sky?
(Summer)
Intermediate and Senior

SPACE: Meeting place.

EQUIPMENT: A set of cards each bearing a constellation is necessary for the playing of this game. They are quickly and easily made.

PROCEDURE: Spread the constellation cards on the floor in their correct relative positions. Then ask the teams in turn questions such as the following, or similar ones based on their work with stars.

In what constellation is the reddest star in the sky?
What does Cassiopeia look like in summer (or winter)?
What birds are there in the sky?
Which little stars are used as a test of good eyesight?
What is the Milky Way?
Which is the brightest, coldest-looking star in the sky?
Who is it that winds himself in between the Great and the Little Bear?
What constellation represents the inventor of the plow?
Where can you find Corona Borealis?

What is Aquila and what is its eye called?
Where is the instrument Orpheus used?

In return for the right answer a player may take the constellation card or star card inquired about. Each correct play is a point for the team.

Which Animal?
Intermediate

SPACE: Out-of-doors or meeting place.
FORMATION: Players sit in a circle.
PROCEDURE: The leader gives short, pithy descriptions of several animals and if she has pictures of them she may show them. After an interval of about ten minutes, during which the girls play some active game, they return and sit in teams. The leader asks questions about the animals she has described. These questions should be based on the earlier descriptions and require more than a yes or no answer. The teams consult and the team leader writes down the cooperative answer of the team.

FINISH: A point is scored for each correct answer.

Sample questions:
Is it a cat's track or a dog's that shows claw marks?
What kind of a home does a hare live in?
What little animal's fur can be rubbed either way?
How does a chipmunk carry nuts to its home?

Bird Riddles
Intermediate and Senior

SPACE: Meeting place.
FORMATION: Teams in groups.
PROCEDURE: The leader gives the following bird riddles and the teams write down their answers.

A bright bird, whose first name is that of a city. *Baltimore Oriole.*
To peddle. *Hawk.*
Less than the whole and a long line of hills. *Partridge.*
The period of darkness, the reverse of out, and a high wind. *Night-in-gale.*
An instrument for driving horses, impecunious, and a boy's name. *Whip-poor-will.*
A monarch and an angler. *King-fisher.*
A boy's nickname, an exclamation, and a part of a chain. *Bob-o-link.*
The bird of imitations. *Mocking bird.*
A tree, an insect product, and part of a bird. *Cedar-wax-wing.*
A young fowl and two letters of the alphabet. *Chick-a-dee.*

Bird Posters
Intermediate and Senior

SPACE: Meeting place.

EQUIPMENT: Four posters. One contains the silhouettes of five birds, the second contains five blocks of colors taken from the coloring of the five birds. On the third are types of songs and foods related to the birds. On the fourth are the pictures of their nests and eggs. The objects in each case should be numbered one to five, but they should not be arranged in the same sequence on each poster. That is, if the robin is the first bird in the silhouette poster, robin's coloring might be the second block of color, his food might be listed third on the third poster, and his nest and eggs placed last on the fourth poster.

PROCEDURE: Each team leader is given a poster and the members of the team decide and write down the names of the five birds that they think are represented on it. They should be written down in order as shown on the poster. After a time limit is reached, all posters are then passed to the next team where the process is repeated until each team has received all four of the posters. The team that has all of the five birds in the correct order for each of the four posters, wins.

VARIATION: The same game may be played with trees; the first poster may show the tree silhouette; the second, twigs and leaves; the third, its economic uses; and the fourth, the flower and fruit.

The same may also be played with fewer posters. In this case the leader describes some of the items, mixing the sequences as in using posters.

Dash
Intermediate

SPACE: Out-of-doors.

NOTE: This game may be used for:

A. Plants having medicinal qualities, such as bittersweet, sundew, monkshood, anemone, boneset.

B. Plants that are good to eat, such as dandelion, milkweed, ferns, cress, mustards, Indian lettuce.

C. Foreign weeds, such as burdock, butter and eggs, purslane.

D. Runaways from our gardens, such as artichokes, ground ivy, oyster plant, chickory, self-heal.

E. Plants with a fly-away seed or with shooting or stick-tight seeds. Many other variations of this game will occur to any leader.

PROCEDURE: Give the girls five minutes for observing nature objects nearby. The leader calls "Bring me a leaf from an edible plant." At the signal, all (or number ones) dash off to find the desired object. The first player to return with one scores a point for her team. This may be used for indoor meetings when girls may give names or find pictures of objects.

I Am Thinking

Brownie and Intermediate

SPACE: Meeting place.
FORMATION: Teams in files.
PROCEDURE: The leader says "I am thinking of............" and goes on to describe an animal whose actions can be easily imitated, such as a rabbit, frog, cat. As soon as the number ones in the files recognize the animal they imitate its walk for a definite distance and then go back to their files. Another animal is described and number twos do the imitating, and so on.
FINISH: The team giving the best series of imitations wins.

Flower Authors

Intermediate

SPACE: Meeting place.
EQUIPMENT: A set of forty-eight cards, on twelve of which are the pictures of twelve different flowers; on twelve cards are pictured the leaves; on twelve their family names are given; and on twelve the place and time of the flowers' blooming.
PROCEDURE: Each of four teams is given three slips on each of which a flower name is written; the forty-eight cards are well mixed and divided evenly among the team leaders. The teams select whatever cards it thinks belong to its flowers, and sends one of its members to exchange cards with the next group as needed.
FINISH: The first team to gather all the correct facts about each of its flowers wins.

Bird Habitat

Intermediate and Senior

SPACE: Four areas at one end of the playing space are marked off as representing a wood, a garden, a pond, and fields.
FORMATION: Team are lined up and their members are numbered consecutively
PROCEDURE: The leader calls a number and a bird; the girls of that number in each team run to the area that the bird inhabits. Numbers should not be called in sequence, since it is more fun not to know who the next one will be

FLOWER VARIATION: This game may also be played by having the leader call out the name of a flower and the members of each team run to the place where the flower grows. Labels such as shady wood, sunny hillside, rocks, marshes, and other localities might be used for flowers.

Nature Blindfold
Intermediate and Senior

SPACE: Meeting place.
FORMATION: Teams sit in little groups and must be blindfolded.
PROCEDURE: Team leaders pass around a specimen from a tree or a part of a plant for their teams to identify by touch, smell, or taste or by all three. As the leaf or plant is passed around the group, each member who has had it writes down her answer. Trying to write down the names when blindfolded adds to the fun of the game. Black birch, sassafras, yarrow are good for smell; blueberry and sour grass for taste; and maple and fern for touch.

Seeds of Trees
Intermediate

SPACE: Large room or out-of-doors.
FORMATION: Teams in files, their members numbered consecutively.
PROCEDURE: Leader calls out one of the following: "nuts," "winged seeds," "cones," or "berries." The first number one to run up to the leader and give a correct example scores for her team. Number ones then go to the end of the files and twos have a chance. Examples: leader, "nuts"—answer, "hickory"; leader, "winged seeds"—answer, "ash."

Leaf Cards
Intermediate and Senior

SPACE: Meeting place.
EQUIPMENT: Set of thirty-two leaf prints or pictures of leaves for each group of eight players.
NOTE: To play this game have the girls collect leaves from many varieties of trees. Blueprints or smoke prints may be made from these. A set of such prints might include four kinds of maples; four fruit trees; four pines; four miscellaneous trees, such as sycamore, linden, Judas, or sassafras; four elms— American, cork, winged, and slippery; four willows; four poplars; and four birches.
PROCEDURE: Mix the set of prints carefully and distribute them among the players. The object is to get a complete family of cards or, if only a few

are playing, several families. A player cannot collect a leaf unless she has two of that family in her hand. When her turn comes she may call on any other player for a certain leaf and if that girl has it, she must give it in exchange for another which the player discards. The player first securing her family (or families) wins and the others are fined one point for each miscellaneous card.

Magic Circle
Intermediate

SPACE: Out-of-doors
EQUIPMENT: Piece of rope about thirty feet long.
FORMATION: Teams in files.
PROCEDURE: A section of ground is encircled with the rope. Each team in turn is given two minutes to list all the things it knows within the circle. When all have had their turns, the lists are checked and the team with the greatest number of items wins the round. Another section of ground is encircled and the same procedure is followed. The team with the highest score wins.

Tree Tag
Brownie and Intermediate

SPACE: Wooded place.
PROCEDURE: The leader touches a tree and tells each girl to run and touch one of the same kind. Those who do so score a point for their team. The girls must also be able to name the tree. Instead of touching the tree the leader may hold up a leaf of the tree she wishes the players to find and touch.

Bark Tag Game
Intermediate

SPACE AND EQUIPMENT: A wooded place where there are at least two different varieties of a family of trees and quite a number of each kind.
PROCEDURE: Team leaders choose sides and each side selects a kind of tree as its home bases. Then each member of each side selects an individual tree of this kind. One player from each side is "it" and tries to tag members from the opposing side as they change from tree to tree. The players must keep moving otherwise "it" can put them out. Only one person is allowed at a tree at one time. As soon as a player is tagged, she turns in to help tag the others.
FINISH: The side that succeeds in tagging all the members of the opposing team wins.

NATURE GAMES 73

NOTE: It is customary to play the game twice, exchanging home trees so that each side may have an opportunity to learn both varieties. This game is especially good in teaching the difference between kinds of trees belonging to the same family, such as the red oaks and the white oaks, the soft maple and the hard maple, the shagbark hickory and the pignut hickory, the grey birch and the black birch. For the best results choose fairly large trees whose bark is well formed. This is a good winter game.

Tree Use Game
Intermediate

SPACE: Wooded place.

EQUIPMENT: Set of cards for each team. Upon each is written a use of timber, such as flooring, cabinet making, tool handles, post, ties, paper pulp, firewood.

PROCEDURE: Five minutes are allowed to find and fasten the cards on the trees, the timber of which is used as indicated by the cards.

FINISH: Each tree properly labeled gives a team one point. The team having the most points at the end of five minutes wins.

Leaf Game
Intermediate and Senior

SPACE: Meeting place.

EQUIPMENT: Leader selects typical leaves or needles.

PROCEDURE: Teams stand in facing lines and the leader pins a leaf on the back of each player. The lines then take turns at letting the opposing side study the leaves for a moment or two until all are sure they can identify their individual opponent's leaf. Then each player questions the girl opposite her about the characteristics of the leaf on her own back until she can guess what variety it is.

The questions may be as follows:

Is it a tree, shrub, or vine?

Is it an evergreen or deciduous?

Is it a needle or a leaf?

If it is a needle, how many are there in a group, are they single? How long are they, are they round or flat? How are they arranged on the branch?

If it is a leaf, is it simple or compound? Size of leaf or leaflets? Pinnately or palmately compound? Leaflets sessile or stalked? Shape of leaf or leaflets? Margin of leaf or leaflets? Surface and color of leaf?

Illustration for a hard maple leaf:

Question: Is it a tree, shrub, or vine?

Answer: It is a tree.
Question: Is it evergreen or deciduous?
Answer: Deciduous.
Question: Is it simple or compound?
Answer: Simple.
Question: Is it large or small?
Answer: Large.
Question: What is the shape of the leaf?
Answer: Broad at the base, sharp-pointed, five-lobed, with the ends of the lobe pointed.
Question: How are the veins arranged?
Answer: Palmately veined.
Question: What is the color and surface of the leaf?
Answer: Color medium dark green, slightly lighter underneath. Leaf rather thin.
FINISH: The side that correctly guesses all its leaves wins.
VARIATION: Only such questions as require "yes" or "no" may be asked.

Leaf Drawing
Intermediate

SPACE: Out-of-doors or indoors.
FORMATION: Two or more teams.
EQUIPMENT: Pencil and paper for each player.
PROCEDURE: The leader reads out a list of about six leaves. Each girl draws all the leaves from memory. When all are finished, each team chooses its best drawing. The best drawing from each team is given to the leader who, with the help of the team leaders, chooses the best one submitted.

Opposite and Alternate Twig Game
Intermediate and Senior

SPACE: Wooded place.
EQUIPMENT: Set of cards bearing names of trees—one half with opposite twigs, one half with alternate.
PROCEDURE: Players are divided into two equal teams. One team is called Opposites, meaning that all trees assigned to that side have opposite twigs. The other team is called Alternates, meaning that its trees have alternate twigs.

Each player on the Opposites team is given a card with the name of a tree having opposite twigs and each player on the Alternates team receives a card with the name of a tree having alternate twigs. The players are given ten minutes in which to find their trees and pin their cards on them. One point may be scored for every tree correctly named. The teams then exchange cards and play another round.

Tree Silhouettes
Brownie and Intermediate

SPACE: Out-of-doors.

EQUIPMENT: Pencil and paper for each player.

PROCEDURE: Call the players' attention to the distinctive outline of some tree easily observed from the camping place or troop room. Suggest that everyone look at it carefully for a few moments and then, turning their backs to it, draw the tree's outline. Have the girls compare their drawings with the silhouette of the tree and criticize them. Some time later let them draw the same outline again and compare it with the original attempt.

True or False*
Intermediate and Senior (may be adapted for Brownies)

PROCEDURE: One person reads the following statements and the players write "true" or "false" on their papers. The players exchange papers and check them with the answers as the leader reads them. Correct answers, together with some additional information for the leader, are given at the end of these statements.

STATEMENTS:
1. The rabbit washes its face with both paws at once.
2. The house mouse uses its tail in climbing.
3. A bat is blind.
4. A bat is a bird.
5. A dog's track shows the claw marks.
6. Goats eat tin cans.
7. Male sheep (rams) fight by striking with head and horns.
8. A cow has front teeth on both jaws.
9. A snake swallows its young in case of danger.
10. All plants growing in the house should be watered twice daily.
11. Goldfish should be kept in the sun and without plants in the bowl or tank.
12. Lead is used as a base in house paint.
13. Onions are bulbs and belong to the lily family.
14. Potatoes are bulbs.

*True or False, Girl Scouts, Inc., Catalog No. 20-202, 10 cents, contains an additional hundred statements.

15. All celery is naturally white.
16. The plant of the vanilla bean is an orchid.
17. The poison oak is a tree.
18. Some kinds of trees have the female flowers on one tree and the male flowers on another.
19. Frog's eggs are enclosed in a jellylike mass when laid.
20. Tulips are native to Turkey and Persia.
21. Whales are mammals and nurse their young.
22. The North Star is the brightest star in the sky.
23. Gold is usually found in quartz.
24. All grasshoppers are wingless when they are young.
25. All moths and butterflies were caterpillars once.
26. Only the male mosquito "bites."
27. All ants are wingless creatures.
28. Practically all insects are harmless to man.
29. A snail's eyes are on the end of stalks. These are sometimes called horns.
30. A turtle sheds its shell every five years.
31. All fishes have scales.
32. There is a star called Venus.
33. If kept in water for some time a horse hair will turn into a worm.
34. Birds have hollow bones.
35. The garden asparagus has been a table vegetable for more than 2,000 years.
36. The ladybug is a beetle.
37. The firefly is a beetle.
38. No elephant has ever seen his own tail.
39. Linen is made from the cotton plant.
40. A school blackboard is made of shale.
41. The largest animal in the world is a whale.
42. The largest bird in the world is the ostrich.
43. A baby chicken pecks its own way out of its shell.
44. Copper is the greatest conductor of electricity.
45. A horse sleeps lying on its side.
46. A sponge is a plant.
47. All snakes are poisonous.
48. The female lion has a mane.
49. Penguins are found at the North and South Poles.
50. Mercury is a mineral.
Count two points for every correct answer.

NATURE GAMES

ANSWERS FOR TRUE AND FALSE STATEMENTS:
1. **True.** Can you think of any difference in the structure of a cat and a rabbit that would make it easier for one of them to sit up on the hind legs for a length of time? Remember, a cat washes its face using one paw at a time.
2. **True.** Its tail is probably an aid in jumping also. What is the tail like? Any fur on it? How does a mouse wash its tail?
3. **False.** A bat is not blind but cannot see very well in the bright light. Where do bats live?
4. **False.** A bat is a mammal—it has fur and nurses its young. What do bats eat?
5. **True.** Why don't claw marks show in a cat's track?
6. **False.** What do goats eat? Why do they like to climb?
7. **True.** Did you ever hear of a "battering ram"? It is an old war weapon fashioned after the sheep's head.
8. **False.** A cow has front teeth only on the lower jaw. How can it cut grass? How does a horse cut grass?
9. **False.** Do snakes lay eggs?
10. **False.** Some should be watered twice a day, some once, some every other day, and some once a week or so. The amount of water depends upon the kind of plant and the amount of sun it gets.
11. **False.** All fish kept in the house should have plants in the water and should not have strong sunlight at any time of the day. Do all fish have teeth?
12. **True.** Lead is also used to make pipes, gutters, bullets, and so on. The United States produces about one half the world's supply of lead. What other country produces lead?
13. **True.** The bulb is the resting stage of the plant and contains food for it when growth is resumed. How many other bulbs can you name?
14. **False.** The potato is a tuber. A tuber is a short, fleshy stem bearing minute scale leaves with buds or eyes in their axils. Sprout the eye of a potato and watch both leaves and buds!
15. **False.** It is blanched by banking the stems with soil and boards. No plant can manufacture green coloring matter without light and sun (either or both). Place a small board on the grass for a few days and see what happens.
16. **True.** Vanilla is a climbing orchid native to Mexico and Central America. How many orchids native to your vicinity do you know? Take good care of them!

17. *False.* Poison oak is a shrub and belongs to the same genus as the poison ivy. No oak trees are poisonous.
18. *True.* The ash tree is one of these. The birch is an example of one that has male and female flowers on the same tree.
19. *True.* Toad's eggs are enclosed in strings of jelly.
20. *True.* Tulip bulbs were first brought to the Netherlands by the Dutch Ambassador to Turkey.
21. *True.* From what part of the whale does whalebone come?
22. *False.* The brightness of a star is called its magnitude. Stars from the first to the sixth magnitude are visible to the naked eye. The North Star is one of the second magnitude.
23. *True.* Sometimes gold is found in stream beds, in sand and gravel, and even sea beaches. It is then called placer gold.
24. *True.* Each time the grasshopper's skin is shed in growing, the wing pads get larger. A few kinds never do get wings but very few.
25. *True.* All caterpillars are vegetarians. All moths and butterflies, if they eat at all, feed upon nectar.
26. *False.* It is the female mosquito that "bites." The male feeds upon plant juices. It is smaller than the female and has feathery antennae.
27. *False.* There are males, sexual females, and modified females. These latter rarely reproduce and are the workers. There are usually several kinds of worker, which are the ones we most often see. Usually once a year the sexual forms are produced and they are fully winged.
28. *True.* Less than twenty per cent of the insects are classed as harmful.
29. *True.* The common garden slug is a shell-less snail.
30. *False.* A turtle's shell is really an enlarged rib and, of course, can never be shed.
31. *False.* Remember the mackerel and catfish. How many more can you think of?
32. *False.* Venus is a planet. How many other planets can you name?
33. *False.* There are many such beliefs about things in nature.
34. *True.* This is one of the things that makes it possible for birds to fly.
35. *True.* Why not try to discover how long some other common garden vegetables have been under cultivation?
36. *True.* The ladybug is very beneficial because the diet of both larva and adult is largely plant lice.
37. *True.* The light of the firefly is the purest light in the world.
38. *True.* The elephant's tail is short, the body broad, and the neck short.
39. *False.* Linen is made from the flax plant, whose Latin name is Linum.

40. *False.* The best type of blackboard is made of slate. Slate is metamorphosed shale. By metamorphosed we mean it has been subjected to heat and pressure.
41. *True.* The sperm whale is the largest animal in the world. Sometimes it grows to be eighty feet in length.
42. *True.* The ostrich is sometimes eight feet high and weighs 300 pounds.
43. *True.* The chick chips his shell with the help of an "egg-tooth."
44. *False.* Silver is 100 per cent conducting—copper 93 per cent.
45. *True.* In rising, the horse lifts his front legs first.
46. *False.* A sponge is a colony of very tiny animals.
47. *False.* Very few snakes are poisonous, and they all, of course, have a very definite place in nature.
48. *False.* The male lion has the mane.
49. *False.* Penguins are found only at the South Pole.
50. *True.* Every mineral is liquid at a certain temperature. Mercury is one that is liquid at a low temperature.

Game of Touch
Brownie, Intermediate, and Senior

SPACE: Indoors or out-of-doors.

PROCEDURE: Players sit in a close circle. Nature objects are passed around from person to person behind the back. After all objects have been passed, each person tries to write down the different objects that passed through her hands. *No peeking!* One point is allowed for each correct answer.

Here are some objects that could be used:
Onion and other kinds of vegetables
Pine cones (two different kinds)
Lump sugar
Oak leaf
Piece of hemlock
Acorn

The Rogues' Gallery
Brownie, Intermediate, and Senior

EQUIPMENT: Paper and pencil for each player.

PROCEDURE: In advance the name of one of the objects listed below is written on a piece of paper for each player. The players are given five minutes in which to sketch what is on the slip of paper.

Shark	Horse
Robin	Goldfish

Skunk
Elm tree
Violet (with leaves!)
Dog (any kind)
Toadstool with toad
Swan
Pig
Turtle

At the end of the time limit hang up the sketches and let the players vote for the best drawn and the funniest.

Nature Steps
Brownie, Intermediate, and Senior

SPACE: Playing area at least fifteen feet deep.

FORMATION: Players stand in a single row, with "it" placed about fifteen feet in front of them.

PROCEDURE: "It" says, "I am thinking of a (bird, flower, tree, mammal, or whatever) whose name begins with 'A' (for instance)." Each person thinks of something and takes as many steps toward "it" as there are letters in the name she has thought of. If a player cannot think of a name, she takes as many steps toward "it" as there are letters in the word "nothing." When all have moved forward, each gives her word or indicates that she moved forward on "nothing." Then "it" gives the word she had in mind. All those who have given the same word are allowed to move back to the line in safety. On signal, "it" then chases the other players and if she tags a player that person becomes "it."

Do You Know?
Intermediate and Senior

EQUIPMENT: Typed copies of the following statements, or similar ones, and pencils.

PROCEDURE:

Underline the correct word:
1. Grass grows from—slips—seeds—bulbs.
2. Tulips grow from—slips—seeds—bulbs.
3. Geraniums grow from—slips—seeds—bulbs.
4. Plants drink water through the—flower—leaves—roots.
5. Nectar comes from the—flower—leaves—roots.
6. Plants breathe through the—flower—leaves—roots.

Underline the word that tells the color:
1. Lily—white—brown—gray.
2. Grass—red—green—pink.
3. Daffodil—black—yellow—blue.
4. Geranium—purple—green—red.
5. Narcissus—white—purple—pink.

FINISH: The girl who first completes her list correctly wins.

What?

Intermediate and Senior

SPACE: Any space where players can write.
EQUIPMENT: Pencils and papers prepared like the following chart, with all but the first column left blank.
PROCEDURE: About ten minutes are allowed after the papers have been distributed for players to fill in the blanks. Players score their own papers, getting one point for every blank correctly filled.

	Animal	What is the female called?	What is the young called?	What is the home called?
1	Pig	Sow	Shoat	Sty
2	Swan	Swan	Cygnet	Nest
3	Fox	Vixen	Pup	Den
4	Elephant	Cow	Calf	Tent or jungle
5	Tiger	Tigress	Kitten	Den
6	Rabbit	Doe	Bunny	Burrow, hutch
7	Sheep	Ewe	Lamb	Fold, pen
8	Deer	Doe	Fawn	Thicket
9	Lion	Lioness	Cub	Den
10	Seal	Cow	Pup	Rocks
11	Horse	Mare	Colt, foal, filly	Barn or plains
12	Eagle	Eagle	Eaglet	Eyrie

What's in the Sky?

Intermediate and Senior

SPACE: Meeting place.
EQUIPMENT: Stars cut from cardboard.
FORMATION: Teams in files.
PROCEDURE: A number of stars are placed in front of each file. The leader holds up a card on which the stars of a constellation are placed in their right positions, and gives the players a few moments in which to study it. Or, she may simply call out the name of a constellation.

Number one of each file picks up a star, puts it in place as the first star in the constellation, and runs to the end of the line. The next person in line puts the second star in place, and so on.

FINISH: The team that first completes the constellation correctly scores a point.

Nature Pictures

Intermediate

SPACE: Large room or out-of-doors.
FORMATION: Players, divided into teams, stand in a circle.
EQUIPMENT: Pins, pencil and paper, and one picture of some nature object for each person in the group. Pictures may be cut from a magazine or seed catalog and should not have the name visible.
PROCEDURE: The leader pins a picture on the back of each player. At a given signal the players break the circle and try to see how many of the pictures they can identify, writing the names on paper. Each player tries to keep the others from seeing her picture, but she may not hide it by leaning against anything. When the leader signals that the time is up, each girl counts the number of objects she has identified and the correct list is read aloud.

FINISH: The team that identifies the greatest number of objects correctly wins.

CHAPTER 8

CROSS-COUNTRY AND STALKING GAMES

THE GAMES IN THIS SECTION develop the scouting skills that have always been associated with trail layers, campers, and pioneers. They help develop self-reliance, self-control, and keen powers of observation. They are especially appropriate for use on hikes, at outdoor meetings, or in camp. Each one may be adapted to fill a special setting, or amplified as a part of a dramatic story.

Stalking means the ability to move about out-of-doors as quietly and as inconspicuously as possible. While our pioneer forefathers needed this skill for hunting and scouting trips, we need it today for full enjoyment of outdoor life. No true camper or nature lover tramps noisily over the countryside, seeing little but frightening away all the creatures of the fields and woods.

Stalking games provide incentive for learning new ways of self-control and patience. The fun in most of these games depends on sure-footedness, swift, quiet action, and a keen eye. They should be played over and over again to develop these skills.

Certain ones, such as "Deer Stalking," "Bird Stalking," "Make No Noise," "Stalking Leader," or "Advancing Statues," are good practice games for beginning stalkers of any age. Advanced games, such as "India Treasure Hunt," "Dispatch Running," and "A Flag Raid," are capable of great variation in presentation, but are based on the general principle of stalking, and the fact that a player who is noisy or exposes herself to full view is liable to be "shot," "scalped," or "killed," and thus becomes a dead loss to her side.

Since these are in a sense dramatic games, specific details as to the rules for playing or scoring are omitted in many cases. It is better for the troop to work out necessary details adapted to its own countryside and players before it starts to play.

Outdoor Judges
Intermediate and Senior

SPACE: Out-of-doors.
FORMATION: Group divided into several teams.
EQUIPMENT: Paper and pencil for each player.
PROCEDURE: Girls follow the leader. At short intervals the leader calls out, "How long?" or "How high?" or "How much does it weigh?" or "How far from this tree to the brook?" and so on, pointing at some object or dis-

tance. Each player jots down what she judges the answer to be. When they have played for a time the girls with the highest score in each team compete in a "final" led by the leader, the winner scoring points for her team. At the same time the other members of the teams have a "final" organized by the team leaders.

Raiders

Intermediate and Senior

SPACE: Out-of-doors.

FORMATION: Two teams, each with eight to twenty players, have bases located about thirty feet apart. A clearly marked line is drawn halfway between the two bases.

PROCEDURE: The two bases contain an equal number of flags or other trophies. The object of the game is for each team in turn to try to break through the enemy's defenses and capture as many flags as possible. If caught by an opponent, the prisoner is conducted to the enemy's base and interned there. Prisoners may be captured only when they are in hostile territory.

FINISH: When both teams have had a chance at invasion, points may be scored for captives and captured trophies.

Famous Game of Tails

Intermediate and Senior

SPACE: Out-of-doors.

FORMATION: Two teams, each with a home about twenty paces from a central spot.

EQUIPMENT: Twenty or thirty small objects, such as stones, horse chestnuts, acorns, seed pods, and so forth. A large handkerchief or tie for each player.

PROCEDURE: The objects are placed close together halfway between the two teams. Each player has a "tail," a tie or large handkerchief, put through her belt in the back but not tied. On signal all players rush to the center and try to seize one bit of treasure and take it safely home without being "detailed" by a player from the other team. If a player loses her tail she must return to her home and watch until the game is over. A player may take but one object at a time and carry it home and leave it before attempting another trip.

FINISH: When all the objects have been removed from the center, the team leaders collect their gains and count up the score. Each player who still has her tail counts five, each tail captured counts five, and each bit of treasure counts one.

Halfway Round and Home Again

Intermediate and Senior

SPACE: Out-of-doors.

FORMATION: Players divided into two teams.

PROCEDURE: Teams start from a given base. One team goes in one direction and the other in another, circling around until they meet halfway at a designated spot. As they advance in this half circle, each side lays a trail backward, burying a treasure at a spot close to the starting point. When the two sides meet they follow each other's trail back home and share the treasures, if they are edible.

All kinds of directions may be used: woodcraft signs, nature signs, compass directions, heights, weights, and distance judging. For example, "If the next tree is fifty feet high, go ten feet northeast; if it is twenty feet, go forty feet south."

Woodcraft Signs

Intermediate and Senior

SPACE: Out-of-doors.

FORMATION: Teams in files.

PROCEDURE: The team captains stand facing their teams at some distance from them, provided with stones, twigs, and grasses. On signal the first player in each team runs up and makes a trail sign. She runs back and touches off the second girl who comes and adds a second sign. The third adds another, and so forth until in the end a small trail has been laid by each team. The team captain checks on mistakes.

FINISH: The team that first finishes a correctly laid trail wins.

VARIATION: Each girl runs up and makes whatever trail sign the team captain calls for. The team captain checks on correctness and destroys each sign before the next girl gets there.

Rescued Prisoners

Intermediate

SPACE: Out-of-doors.

FORMATION: Group is divided into prisoners and rescuers, with twice as many rescuers as prisoners. Two or three girls may volunteer to tie up the prisoners instead of taking part.

PROCEDURE: The prisoners are bound hand and foot at some distance from the home base. On signal the rescuers run from home base in pairs to the aid of the prisoners. The first pair to arrive home with an unbound prisoner scores for its team.

Hare and Hounds Up to Date
Brownie, Intermediate, and Senior

Instead of having the hare leave behind a trail of paper, she makes her trail of a certain kind of leaf that is agreed upon by all of the players—or of white pebbles or any other little objects by which she can be trailed. It isn't good Girl Scouting to litter up a countryside with paper. Better still, use trail signs or arrows scratched in the sand, on the ground, or formed by dead twigs. . .

Sardines
Intermediate and Senior

SPACE: Out-of-doors, a large but definitely understood area.

FORMATION: The group is divided into two teams, plus one member chosen to be the fugitive.

PROCEDURE: One girl chosen to be a fugitive is given five minutes in which to hide. Then the other players start out individually to find her. When one girl finds the fugitive she joins her in her hiding place. When discovered by the next player, the three become fugitives, and so on until all have discovered the hidden party.

FINISH: The first four girls to join the fugitive score for their teams.

NOTE: This game may also be played indoors with hilarious results.

Sealed Orders
Intermediate and Senior

SPACE: Meeting place.

FORMATION: Group is divided into equal teams. The teams are given names and the members of each are numbered beginning with one.

EQUIPMENT: Any items needed to carry out the assignments given, which should be based on the current interests of the group.

PROCEDURE: A list of assignments, equal in number to the size of the teams, is made out. Each set is folded and hidden somewhere in the room, after writing the team's name on it. Each team must find its own set of orders and then begin at once to carry out the assignments, number one has assignment one, and so on.

FINISH: The team that finishes its assignments first gets four points.

The second team gets three points.

The third team gets two points.

In addition, the team that does the best work should get six points.

Sample list of assignments:
1. Find out the length of the troop room.
2. Draw an American Flag.
3. Name three kinds of tinder for starting a fire for outdoor cooking.
4. Draw a recognizable sketch of some familiar animal or plant.
5. Name four services that your community provides for its citizens.
6. Wrap up three books, making a neat parcel.

Shipwrecked Travelers
Intermediate and Senior

SPACE: An outdoor place with definitely set boundaries.
FORMATION: The group is divided into couples.
PROCEDURE: Each couple is given a list of the following requirements, which must be filled within a certain time limit:
Find something edible.
Find something to wear.
Find material to be used in constructing a house.
Find material for thatching a roof.
Find material from which a weapon can be made.
Find something that can be used for a tool.
FINISH: The first couple to complete its list wins.

How Many Miles to Babylon?
Brownie and Intermediate

SPACE: Out-of-doors.
FORMATION: Players stand in a long line, side by side, holding hands. The two players at one end hold their clasped hands up to form a gate without breaking from the line.
PROCEDURE: The player at the opposite end circles around to the gate, followed by the rest of the line still holding hands. Upon reaching the gate she asks:
"How many miles to Babylon?"
"Three score and ten," reply the gate keepers.
"Shall we get there by candle-light?" inquires the leader.
"Yes, and back again."
The leader then goes through the gate, pulling the line after her. When the last girl is through, the line breaks and the players scatter. The gate keepers quickly loose hands and give chase, catching as many players as they can. The first and last players caught take their turn at forming the gate.

Poison

Brownie and Intermediate

SPACE: Large room or out-of-doors.

PROCEDURE: Chalk a small circle on the floor. The players join hands around it and everyone tries to make someone else put a foot inside. Anyone that touches the circle is "poisoned" and must endeavor to catch one of the other players before she can touch the wall designated as a safety base. If she succeeds, her captive must drop out. If she catches no one, she must drop out. The players join hands again, and the fun continues until only one player—or none—remains.

Chariot Race

Intermediate

SPACE: Large playing area.

FORMATION: Twelve players are needed for one race. Several races may be run simultaneously if there are many playing. Four of the twelve players serve as "corner posts" for a ten-foot square around which the race is to take place. Two chariots—each formed by four players locking arms—line up beside two diagonal posts, facing in the same direction around the course. On signal, both chariots begin to run forward around the four corners of the square trying to overtake one another.

FINISH: The chariot that succeeds in overtaking (touching) the other wins the race. If there are several pairs of chariots, the winners of the different races may run against one another.

Three Around

Intermediate

SPACE: Out-of-doors.

FORMATION: Players first form a single circle in which they count off by threes. Number ones remain in their places in the circle, number twos stand behind ones, and number threes behind twos. The spokes of the wheel thus formed must be equal with an extra player chosen to be "it." "It" runs around the outside of the wheel and finally tags some number three at the outer end of a spoke. This number three tags number two in front of her, number two tags number one and all three players then run around the wheel to the right. "It" steps into number one's place. The last member of the running spoke to return to the starting point will be without a place and becomes "it" for the next round.

The counting off may be by twos if the group is small, or up to fives or sixes if there are many players.

Beat Around
Brownie and Intermediate

SPACE: Out-of-doors.

FORMATION: Single circle facing in.

PROCEDURE: One person is "it" with a rolled-up newspaper or something suitable to swat another player. "It" runs around outside of circle and places swatter in hands of any member of the circle. "It" steps in her place. The person on the right of the player who now has the swatter runs around the circle chased by the person who has the swatter who in turn tries to swat the runner as many times as possible back to place. The person holding the swatter then is "it" next time, and so on.

Deer Stalking
Intermediate

SPACE: Out-of-doors or indoors.

FORMATION: The group, designated as two teams, deer and stalkers, sits in a large circle around a table placed in the center. Two players are chosen to be "deer" and "stalker."

PROCEDURE: The deer and stalker are blindfolded. They are placed at opposite ends of a large table in the center of the circle and at a given moment begin moving about. The stalker's business is, of course, to catch the deer within a given time limit, and the deer's to avoid being caught, but neither must run into the players sitting in the circle. Absolute silence should be kept both by the audience and players. If the stalker succeeds in catching the deer within the time limit, her team is given one point. If not, the deer's team gains a point. In either case, each of the two players chooses a member of her team to take her place, and the game continues for several rounds.

Bird Stalking
Intermediate

SPACE: Large room.

EQUIPMENT: Two correctly colored pictures of birds for each team of four to six players.

PROCEDURE: A girl from each team sits on a chair at one end of the room, holding a picture of a bird in each hand. They are birds in a wood. The chairs should be some distance apart. The rest of the players creep up quietly to observe the birds closely. If they make a noise, the keeper of the wood, who may be the leader or a girl chosen as keeper, "shoots" them, and they can proceed no further. When every stalker has had an opportunity to observe all of the birds, each team returns to its corner and makes a list of the birds observed, adding descriptions if desired. The team that has the most complete list and most accurate descriptions wins. The description alone might count one, and the name and description two.

Make No Noise
Brownie and Intermediate

SPACE: Large room.

FORMATION: Players, divided into two teams, sit in a large circle. One girl from each team is chosen to sit in the center of the circle, facing the half circle formed by the opposing team.

PROCEDURE: The two girls within the circle are blindfolded and each has a handkerchief slipped through the back of her belt for a tail.

The players in the center point toward the team in front of them and the girls pointed at creep forward and try to secure the tail of their opponent without being heard. If a player in the center hears a sound, she points in its direction. If she aims directly at a girl who is trying to secure either her own or her opponent-partner's tail the player must return to her place.

FINISH: The first player to secure a tail wins a point for her team and becomes the pointer for her side.

Stalking Leader
Brownie and Intermediate

SPACE: Out-of-doors.

FORMATION: Players facing outward make a ring around the leader.

PROCEDURE: They then advance about fifty yards and camouflage themselves as effectively as possible. At a given signal they start to creep back to the center. Their object is to get in as close as possible to the leader without being seen. The leader is allowed to turn around as much as she likes but not to move from the center. This can also be played by having the leader call out a girl's name if she sees her move at all. If the girl is motionless then she cannot be seen.

FINISH: When the whistle blows, the girls stand up where they are and the nearest score points for their patrols.

VARIATION: When the players have an inkling of stalking, the game may be made more complicated. During the time when the girls are creeping up, the leader may be performing a series of actions such as dancing, yawning, writing. Then the players should not only stalk the leader but see and remember all of the things that she does without being seen themselves. As soon as the leader recognizes anyone she calls her name and the player must lie down dead where she is or go quietly up to the center and watch the stalking. The list of actions may be made individually or teams may get together at the end of the game and consult about them.

Advancing Statues
Brownie and Intermediate

SPACE: Out-of-doors.

GROUND MARKS: Two lines about twenty feet apart.

FORMATION: All players stand back of a given line; the leader stands on the other, her back to the troop.

PROCEDURE: From time to time the leader turns round to look at the players. When the leader is not looking each player advances, her aim is to reach the leader's line without being seen to move. When the leader is looking she stands like a statue. Upon seeing the slightest move the leader tells that person to go back to the starting line.

FINISH: The team first reaching the goal line wins the game.

Ghosts
Intermediate and Senior

SPACE: Out-of-doors.

PREPARATION: The leader stations about half a dozen Girl Scouts well camouflaged along the trail or walk.

PROCEDURE: The rest walk along the trail and see how many figures they can distinguish. They usually conjure up many that are not there. After playing this game once or twice, withdraw the figures and lead the girls around an empty area. It is wonderful how many "ghosts" they will see.

Indian Treasure Hunt
Intermediate and Senior

SPACE: Woods.

FORMATION: Two teams, the reds and the blues, the players of each numbered consecutively.

EQUIPMENT: Bits of cardboard or thin bark, pencils or charcoal, lengths of string for each player and some object to serve as a treasure.

PROCEDURE: Each player writes her number and color on a piece of cardboard and ties it around her forehead so that the number is directly in front.

The red team goes forth to lay a trail and hide the treasure. After a certain period of time the blues start out on the trail, following trail signs. The team following the trail tries to find the treasure without having any of its players "scalped." When a member of either team can identify an opponent by calling out her correct number, the identified player must turn over her numbered forehead band as a trophy for the other side. She is then considered "scalped" and does not participate further in the hunt.

FINISH: Each captured "scalp" counts ten points for the side that takes it and the finding—or keeping—of the treasure counts twenty-five points. This treasure hunt may properly end with a war dance by the victors.

Dispatch Running
Intermediate and Senior

SPACE: An outdoor place that provides cover.

FORMATION: Two teams—dispatch runners and the enemy.

PROCEDURE: One team writes out dispatches that are to be carried by each player to the team leader, who is stationed at a secret "fort." Each player hides her dispatch somewhere about her person. The members of the enemy team, who are scattered beyond the starting line, try to intercept the dispatch runners by stalking them. If a dispatch runner is caught, her captors may have ten guesses as to where the dispatch is hidden. If the captors cannot locate the hidden message in ten guesses, the captive is released and allowed to proceed. A dispatch runner who reaches her fort without being caught makes two points; if she is caught but the hiding place of the message is not guessed, one point. The enemy team makes two points for each captive whose message they locate by guesses, one point for each captive whose message is not secured.

Treasure: A Flag Raid
Intermediate and Senior

SPACE: A definite area of about eighty yards clearly understood by all of the players and providing a certain amount of cover.

FORMATION: Two bands of players.

PREPARATION: Each side hides its treasures, and each team must have an idea where the other's treasure is hidden. It may be in a certain tree on the back line of the plot, or it may be a flag flaunting merrily in the breeze.

GROUND MARKS: A base line for each team.

PROCEDURE: At a given signal, the teams hide the treasure and at another signal, the attack begins. Each team should appoint a captain, who organizes her Girl Scouts to attack, defend, and observe. Defense should not be al-

CROSS-COUNTRY AND STALKING GAMES

lowed nearer than about ten yards to the treasure. The object is to seize the enemy's treasure and get all the way home with it. "Killing" is best done by calling the person's name or number. Other rules can be made by the players as they think fit. At the end of the game, points are added up. Each "dead" might count five and each bit of treasure, ten. Or if the treasure is just the one flag, it might count twenty.

Will-o'-the-Wisp
Intermediate and Senior

SPACE: Out-of-doors in the evening.

EQUIPMENT: Lantern or flashlight.

FORMATION: Two teams who are the pursuers and two lantern bearers who are the will-o'-the-wisps.

PROCEDURE: The two lantern bearers sets off in a given direction with a lighted lantern or a flashlight. After two minutes have passed the two teams start in pursuit. The lantern bearer must show her light at least every two minutes, concealing it the rest of the time. The two take turns in carrying it and so may relieve each other in difficulties but either may be captured. The one without the light can often mingle with the pursuers without being recognized and warn her partner from time to time. They should arrange a series of secret calls between them.

FINISH: The team that overtakes the will-o'-the-wisps wins.

Circles
Intermediate and Senior

SPACE: Out-of-doors. This game is best played in a place that offers a certain amount of cover, but it may be varied with a little ingenuity to suit the country available. It is huge fun played at twilight.

FORMATION: Players form a rather close circle around a "spotter" with a whistle and two "fetchers."

PROCEDURE: Upon signal all players in the circle run outward to some distance, still keeping a rough circle formation. At a whistle signal from the spotter, they stop and face toward the center, each at some distance from the other. With her eyes closed, the spotter gives a long whistle and the wide circle moves inward. With eyes still closed the spotter gives a short whistle and they stop and drop into cover. After the short whistle signal the spotter counts to five and opens her eyes to make a careful survey of the country to see if she can spot any players. The fetchers, at her direction, bring in those that are seen to the center of the circle where they become inactive. Proceeding in this manner the circle gradually gets nearer to the central point.

The first three players to be "fetched" become the spotter and fetchers for the next round.

Apache Relay Race
Intermediate and Senior

SPACE: Out-of-doors.

FORMATION: The leader is posted at one end of a half mile stretch and the assistant leader at the other end of this distance. In between the eight players of two competing bands are posted about 110 yards apart. The leader gives the first runner of each band a verbal message that requires an answer. On signal the first runners deliver the message to the next in line, and so on. The last runner must write the message down and deliver it to the assistant who sends a verbal reply by each band of runners. When this reply reaches the first runner, she writes it down and delivers it to the leader.

FINISH: The band that first delivers the correct return message to the leader wins the race.

Hats and Pebbles
Intermediate

SPACE: Out-of-doors.

PROCEDURE: Ten or twelve players place their hats (hollows up) in a row near the side of a house, a fence, a log, or a line. A deadline is drawn ten feet in front of the hats, behind which all must stand. One player begins by trying to toss a soft ball into one of the hats. Every time she misses a hat, a pebble is put into her own and she tries again.

As soon as she drops the ball into a hat, the owner of the hat is "it" and runs to get the ball; all the rest run away. "It" must not follow beyond the deadline, but must throw the ball at someone. If she hits a player, a pebble goes into that person's hat; if not, a pebble goes into "it's" hat. The players line up again and "it" begins the play again. As soon as a player has five pebbles in her hat she must pay a forfeit or perform some stunt called for by "it."

The Lost Patrol
Intermediate and Senior

SPACE: Out-of-doors.

FORMATION: Players are divided into two teams.

PROCEDURE: A goal and a signal station are decided upon. The members of one team are called searchers. The other team is called the Lost Patrol. The captain of the Lost Patrol hides all of her players in the same place. She then goes to the signal station and signals the searchers to begin the search.

CROSS-COUNTRY AND STALKING GAMES

The searchers start out separately or in groups as directed by their captain. At intervals, the captain of the Lost Patrol, who remains at the signal station, tells her players by means of signals previously agreed upon where the searchers are. When the searchers are at a safe distance, she signals her team to return to the goal, at the same time calling, "Lost Patrol!" The searchers immediately start to chase the Lost Patrol. If the Patrol reaches the goal first, it wins the game and may hide again. If any one of the searchers discovers the hiding team, she calls, "Lost Patrol," and they all start to race for the goal. If the searchers reach the goal first, they win and become the Lost Patrol, and the game is repeated.

Signals may be given by signal flags or whistle, using the Morse Code.

Trailing
Intermediate

SPACE: Out-of-doors.

EQUIPMENT: One hundred and thirty small pieces of paper in two different colors—red and yellow perhaps.

PROCEDURE: Two persons are chosen to be deer. They are given a hundred pieces of red paper and thirty pieces of yellow paper and ten minutes' start. They must lay a track, as crooked as they please, dropping a piece of red paper every three or four yards and a piece of yellow every twenty. After ten minutes, the deer must hide in the same place.

The trailers follow them, picking up the bits of red and yellow paper. Each red piece counts one point, each yellow piece two. The player who finds the deer scores ten points.

Forcing the City Gates
Brownie and Intermediate

SPACE: Out-of-doors.

FORMATION: Players in two teams. Each team joins hands and stands in a straight line facing the other team at a distance of about ten feet.

PROCEDURE: Each line represents the gates of a city. It is advisable to alternate the stronger and weaker players so as to equalize the point of attack. The leader of each side calls upon one of her players to step out of her own line and try to break through or dodge under the hands of the opposing side. Each player may try three times, but if she fails she joins the opposite side. If she succeds, she returns to her side taking with her the two through whom she broke or dodged. The leaders then choose another player to try to force the city gates.

FINISH: The side that has the greatest number of players at the end of designated time is the victor.

CHAPTER 9

SAFETY-WISE GAMES

THIS GROUP OF GAMES may prove interesting to girls who have had some training in first aid, since they furnish a pleasant way to practice some essential points that are usually stressed. They may serve also as an emphasis of safety elements to be included in plans for trips and excursions.

Acting Accidents
Intermediate and Senior

SPACE: Meeting place.
PROCEDURE: One Girl Scout is chosen from each team to act as a patient. She runs to the next team, acts her accident, and has it treated.
FINISH: Points are given for ingenuity of various kinds.
VARIATION: Players are divided into pairs, and an "accident" is called out. The girls who are giving first aid treat the victim as sensibly and quickly as possible.
ANOTHER VARIATION: Suitable "accidents" are written on slips of paper by the leader and drawn by team leaders. The team then dramatizes the one their leader has drawn. The other teams sit and watch the dramatization, taking notes if they like, and at the end of the performance, each team in turn comments on an especially good point or makes a criticism.

Witness
Brownie, Intermediate, and Senior

SPACE: Meeting place.
EQUIPMENT: Two copies (drawn or clipped from a newspaper) of a picture of an accident.
PROCEDURE: Divide group into two teams. Present each group with picture for two minutes. Then take it away and ask a set of questions. The questions should be factual and pertain to what they saw in the picture.
FINISH: The side answering the most questions correctly wins.

Magazine Safety
Intermediate and Senior

SPACE: Meeting place.
EQUIPMENT: Paper and pencil.

PROCEDURE: Give the following list of questions to each team. Five minutes are allowed for answering. The blank space in each statement is to be filled in by the name of a popular magazine.
1. What we should do before crossing the street.................(Look)
2. Play safe if you don't want to lose your.................(Life)
3. A person accustomed to the dangers of New York City......(New Yorker)
4. Safety should be the *friend of every youth*......(*Youth's Companion*)
5. The *Stop Signal Book*...........(*Red Book*)
6. ....is a sure way to have a safe home. (*Good Housekeeping*)
7. Many people lose their lives by rushing and trying to save a little ....(*Time*)
8. A careless driver is a criminal who should be deprived of his freedom and..................(*Liberty*)
9. Swimming in the.................Ocean is fun is we are careful. (*Atlantic*)
10. ....watches over those who practice safety. (*Fortune*)

First Aid Quiz
Brownie, Intermediate, and Senior

SPACE: Meeting place.
FORMATION: Two teams sitting facing each other.
PROCEDURE: The leader of the troop prepares a set of first aid questions beforehand. She asks the first player of team A a question. If she fails to answer she goes to the end of the line on the other side. Then the leader asks the first player of team B a question. The team having the greatest number of players when the contest is over wins.
VARIATION: This may also be used as a "safety-wise quiz."

Bandage Relay
Intermediate and Senior

SPACE: Meeting place.
FORMATION: Divide the group into teams of six or eight depending upon the number of injuries to be bandaged.
PROCEDURE: Place one player in front of each team to act as the victim. Give each player a triangular bandage and assign her a certain part of the body to bandage—head, face, neck, shoulder, elbow, hand, thigh, knee, foot, for example.
One by one the players apply their bandages until all bandages are on.
FINISH: The team having the greatest number of bandages correctly and neatly put on wins. The relay may be played a second time by having each player remove his own bandage. The team finishing first wins.

Emergency

Intermediate and Senior

SPACE: Meeting place.

EQUIPMENT: Slips of paper placed around the room on which names of various kinds of first aid apparatus are written: such as bandages, hot water bottle, blanket.

PROCEDURE: The troop goes around observing these, but does not touch them. Then each team leader is given a slip of paper with some emergency written on it, such as "chill from exposure," "clothes on fire." She runs to her team and they all collect, as quickly as possible, the remedies and the apparatus required. Then the members of the team tell briefly what they would do, handing in the slips of paper as they tell how they would use the apparatus indicated on them.

Health Game

Brownie and Intermediate

SPACE: Meeting place.
EQUIPMENT: Plasticene.
FORMATION: Teams in corners.

PROCEDURE: Each team is given lumps of different colored plasticene and told to illustrate one of the health laws by making a model relating to it. Teams always have amusing ideas of what to make—for instance, tiny models of different kinds of food that make a well balanced meal.

FINISH: When models are all made and inspected, the teams vote on the best one.

Stay on the Highway Relay

Brownie and Intermediate

SPACE: Meeting place.
FORMATION: Teams in files.
EQUIPMENT: A yardstick, penny, toothpick for each team.

PROCEDURE: Each team is outfitted with a yardstick, (to represent a highway) a penny, and a toothpick (colored differently for each team). Each player in turn places the penny on one end of the yardstick and pushes it to the other end of the yardstick and back with the toothpick. If the coin falls off the player must begin again.

FINISH: The first team having traversed the highway wins.

CHAPTER 10

WINTER OUTDOOR GAMES

BEFORE COMPLETING PLANS for a winter outdoor program to be used either on a hike or at camp, look over the games given in other sections. Nature games, cross-country and stalking games may easily be adapted to a winter scene. The games in this section require snow.

Lion Hunting

Intermediate

FORMATION: The group is divided into equal teams, each of which chooses a member to act as the lion.

PROCEDURE: The lions fasten tracking irons (which may be made from tin cans) on their feet and are provided with a pocketful of torn colored paper and six balls (which may be made from newspapers or rags). They are allowed a fifteen- or twenty-minute start. Then the teams go after them, following their trails. Each hunter is armed with one ball. The lions may hide or creep about or run, but whenever the ground is too hard or grassy to show tracks, they must drop a few bits of colored paper every few yards.

When a team comes near to a lion's lair, the lion throws her balls at the hunters and the moment a hunter is hit, she must drop out of the chase. If the lion is hit by a hunter's ball, she is wounded but is not considered captured until hit three times. Balls may be fired only once; they cannot be picked up and fired again. Each person is responsible for collecting her own balls.

FINISH: The first team that captures a lion is the winner.

If there is snow, this game may be placed without tracking irons, and snowballs may be used.

Arctic Expedition

Intermediate and Senior

PROCEDURE: Each team takes a sled or sleigh or toboggan. This may be fitted with harness and pulled by two girls or dogs. Each team has a different destination in mind.

Two members go ahead (with a half-hour start) to open up the way and lay the trail. The remainder of the team follows with the sled, carrying cooking utensils, food, and so forth. They find the way by means of the trail and such signs as the advance players may draw in the snow.

All signs seen on the way are to be noted and their meaning read.

Or, if there is but one sled for the whole group, two members may be sent on ahead to open up the way and lay the trail a half hour in advance of the others. The first team may follow this trail with the provisions on the sled. Other teams follow at intervals. They must note all signs and report on findings.

The first two to arrive gather wood and build a fire. As soon as the provisions arrive, the cooks set about to get the meal while the others build a snow shelter.

For the return trip arrange to have different girls lay the trail back to camp, going by another route.

Fox Hunting
Intermediate

PROCEDURE: This game should be played where there is plenty of untrodden snow about. Two players representing foxes start from the middle of a field or piece of open ground, and five minutes later the rest set out on their trail. The foxes are not allowed to follow any human tracks. If they approach a pathway where other people have been, they must turn off in another direction. They may walk along the top of walls or use any other ruse they like, such as treading in each other's tracks and then one vaulting aside with a staff. Both foxes must be caught by the pursuers within an hour's time in order to count the hunt a success. If the foxes remain in the field for an hour and return safely to the starting point, they are the victors.

Dog Team Race
Intermediate

FORMATION: One member of each team of eight acts as a driver; the others are huskies. Each team is equipped with one sled and seven pieces of rope four feet long.

PROCEDURE: The huskies line up in front of the sled, with the driver in the rear and next to the sled. On signal, the huskies tie their ropes together, and the driver fastens the end of the long line to the sled. The huskies pull the sled with the driver on it to the finish line. If the driver falls from the sled or ropes come untied before the finish line is reached, the team is disqualified.

FINISH: The first team to reach the finish line without mishap wins.

WINTER OUTDOOR GAMES

Snowball Rolling Contest

Brownie and Intermediate

PROCEDURE: A snowball one foot in diameter is allowed each contestant at the start. When the signal is given, balls may be rolled for five minutes. At the end of that time, action must cease.

FINISH: Snowballs are measured through their greatest diameter. The player whose ball measures the most wins the contest.

Snow Sculpture

Brownie, Intermediate, and Senior

PROCEDURE: Allow a specified time for creating figures of the sculptors' own choosing out of snow.

Or, the name of a famous character or a familiar animal may be given to each sculptor who then models her figure accordingly. •

Judges may be appointed or votes taken to determine first, second, and third place.

Winter Track Meet

Brownie, Intermediate, and Senior

1. Snowball throw for accuracy. Teams of four throw at a target. Each hit counts one point.

2. Snowball throw for distance. Teams of four. Each member is allowed one throw. The greatest aggregate distance wins.

3. Skating, skiing, and snowshoeing events are popular if equipment allows and the ice and snow are just right.

4. Relay sleigh race. Teams of nine—one messenger and four pairs of horses. Equipment—one sled with pulling ropes for each team.

> Horses 1 and 2 are stationed at Post A
>
> Horses 3 and 4 are stationed at Post B
>
> Horses 5 and 6 are stationed at Post C
>
> Horses 7 and 8 are stationed at Post D

On signal, the messenger jumps on the sled and is pulled by horses 1 and 2 from Post A to Post B where horses are changed, and so on the length of the course. The horses are changed at each post. All teams travel the same course and the first to finish wins the race.

Scouting

Intermediate

SPACE: Out-of-doors.

PROCEDURE: A number of goals are marked on a map at equal distances from a central point, and the players in pairs or in teams draw straws to select goals. All set out at the same time, go direct to the goal, and return as soon as possible. The last team to return gets zero for traveling. The others count one point for each minute they are ahead of the last team. Points up to a hundred are allowed for the stories of the journey. Or, ten points may be allowed for each rabbit seen, ten for each squirrel, five for each chipmunk, one for each identified bird, two for a cat, one for a dog.

BOOKS FOR THE LEADER OF GAMES

Children's Party Book, The, by Mary Breen (Barnes, 1941, $2.50).
Particularly good for leaders of Brownie and Intermediate troops. It is a how-to-do and how-to-make book of games, decorations, and favors for parties around the year.

Four Hundred Games for School, Home, and Playground by E. F. Acker (F. A. Owens Publishing Company, Dansville, N. Y., 1923, $1.50).

Games and Game Leadership by Charles F. Smith (Dodd, Mead, 1932, $2.50).
Excellent scource for indoor and outdoor games for all age levels.

Games for the Playground, Home, School, and Gymnasium by Jessie H. Bancroft (Macmillan, 1909, $3).
A large collection of games simply and clearly described. Helpful in planning games for all age levels.

Games of Law Organization by Garson Herman (Author, 106 Great Kills Road, Staten Island, N. Y., 50 cents).
Especially helpful to Brownie leaders and Scout leaders who have young Scouts—up to twelve years of age.

Girl Scout Handbook 1940 edition (Girl Scouts, Catalog No. 20-101, 75 cents).
See "Sports and Games," pages 600-657.

Handbook for Recreation Leaders by Ella Gardner (U. S. Department of Labor, Childrens Bureau, Publication No. 231, 25 cents).
Essential for all Girl Scout leaders. Contains leadership material and a collection of games.

Ice-breakers and the Ice-breaker Herself by Edna Geister (Harper, 1924, $1.35).
Useful in planning for parties. Also contains suggestions to leader of games.

One Hundred Amusements for Evening Parties, Picnics and Social Gatherings (Fitzgerald Publishing Co., N. Y., $4).
Material for Senior Girl Scout parties.

Social Games for Recreation by Mason and Mitchell (Barnes, 1935, $2.50).
Contains general suggestions for outdoor programs, campfire gatherings, and troop meeting games.

ALPHABETICAL INDEX OF GAMES

	PAGE
Acting Accidents	96
Actions	19
Advancing Statues	91
Animal Notes	67
Animal Team Race	3
Apache Relay Race	94
Arctic Expedition	99
Arithmetic Game	26
Authors	21
Automobile Race	11
Back-to-Back Tag	11
Backwards Relay	45
Balance Kick	13
Balance Relay	45
Ball Puss	36
Balloon Battle	7
Bandage Relay	97
Bark Tag Game	72
Bean Bag Jerusalem	39
Beat Around	89
Bird Habitat	70
Bird Posters	69
Bird Riddles	68
Bird Stalking	89
Bird's Nest	6
Birds of Prey	66
Blind Man Squat	13
Blotch	66
Bouncing Ball Relay	53
Brownie Chariot Race	30
Brownies and Fairies	30
Buddy Game	4
Bullet Spin	14
Bumps	6
Buzz	5
Camel Strut	14
Camp Equipment	20
Centipedes	44
Chair Sit Relay	49
Chalk Line Relay	46
Chariot Race	88
Circle	38
Circle Change Relay	47
Circle Pass Relay	51
Circle Stride Ball	36

	PAGE
Circles	93
Citizenship Game	18
Collar Tag	10
Come Along	32
Corner Ball	34
Cowboy Relay	54
Crazy Groceries	24
Crosses	5
Dash	69
Deer Stalking	89
Dispatch Running	92
Do You Know?	80
Dodge Ball	37
Dog Team Race	100
Dom Dom	23
Double Heel Click	14
Double Russian Side Step	15
Double Tag	10
Drummer Man	8
Duck Strut	15
Dumb Crambo	22
Eenie, Weenie, Coxie, Wanie	32
Eliza Crossing the Ice	9
Emergency	98
Famous Game of Tails	84
Farmyard	4
Feeling	21
Find a Seat	29
Finger Sight	22
Fish and Net	33
First Aid Quiz	97
Flag Raid, A. *See Treasure.*	
Flower Authors	70
Flower Game	27
Forcing the City Gates	95
Foreign Shopping	12
Fox Hunting	100
Frog in the Sea	31
Game of Touch	79
Getting Acquainted	3
Ghosts	91
Girl Scout Baseball	19
Gossip	9

INDEX

	PAGE		PAGE
Halfway Round and Home Again	85	Nature Squares	63
Hang Tag	10	Nature Steps	80
Hare and Hounds Up to Date	86	Newspaper Costumes	5
Hats and Pebbles	94	Newspaper Race	47
Hawk and Doves	31	Nope	23
Health Game	98	Number Relay	17
Hexapod Questions	64	Obstacle Relay	47
Hidden Quests	64	Old Hen and Chickens	32
Hit the Bat	39	Opposite and Alternate Twig Game	74
Holes	7	Out of Squares Jerusalem	6
How Many Miles to Babylon?	87	Outdoor Judges	83
I Am a Tree	58	Over and Under Relay	50
I Am Thinking	70	Overhead Relay	51
Images	8	Overtake Pass	39
In and Out Relay	48	Pandora's Box	56
Indian Guessing Game	18	Paper Bag Relay	53
Indian Treasure Hunt	91	Partner Relay	45
Indoor Rounders	35	Partner Tag	10
Indoor Trail	56	Pass and Around Relay	48
Jingling	33	Pass and Crawl Relay	51
Jumping Ball	36	Peanut Relay	52
Jumping Rope Relay	52	Penny Game	26
Knot Problem	42	Pictures	21
Knot Relay	42	Place the Stars	65
Leaf Cards	71	Poison	88
Leaf Drawing	74	Progressive Dodge Ball	38
Leaf Game	73	Quicksight	20
Leaf Hunt	61	Rabbits in a Trap	9
Life Line Race	41	Raiders	84
Limber Relay	48	Raisin Relay	53
Lion Hunting	99	Reds and Blues	40
Listening	19	Relay Ball Game	50
Look-See	22	Remembering Shapes	23
Look Sharp	20	Rescue Relay	43
Lost Patrol, The	94	Rescued Prisoners	85
Magazine Safety	96	Ring Game	10
Magic Circle	72	Roadside Cribbage	55
Magic Music	29	Rock Discoveries	65
Make No Noise	90	Rogues' Gallery, The	79
Matching Leaves—I	60	Run Around Relay	43
Matching Leaves—II	60	Running Relay	44
Midnight	31	Salute Relay	46
Milady Goes to Paris	7	Sardines	86
Name the Leaves	62	Scouting	102
Nature Blindfold	71	Sealed Orders	86
Nature Pictures	82	Secret Leaves	58
Nature Puzzles	61	Seeds of Trees	71
		Shipwrecked Travelers	87

	PAGE		PAGE
Shop Window Race	25	Trailing	95
Shuttle Relay	44	Treasure: A Flag Raid	92
Siamese Relay	46	Tree Facts	57
Singing Tag	10	Tree Identification Game	59
Sinking Ships—I	40	Tree Silhouettes	75
Sinking Ships—II	41	Tree Tag	72
Sit and Change Relay	49	Tree Use Game	73
Skip, Run, or Sit	5	True or False	75
Snow Sculpture	101	Turn About Relay	49
Snowball Rolling Contest	101	Twelve o'Clock at Night. *See Midnight.*	
Soccer Dodge Ball	37	Twenty-one Questions	18
Sounds	55	Two in One	59
Spin the Platter	11	Ty's	25
Spud	35		
Squad Dodge Ball	37		
Squat Spring	16	Washington Crosses the Delaware	17
Stalking Leader	90	Watching the Trail	63
Star Pictures	65	What?	81
Stay on the Highway Relay	98	What Letter?	27
Stoop and Stretch Relay	50	What's in the Sky?	82
Story by Tracks, The	57	Which Animal?	68
Subconscious Observation	64	Who's Who in the Sky	67
		Will-o'-the-Wisp	93
Tag Games	10	Winter Track Meet	101
Team Passing	34	Witness	96
Team Treasure Hunt	62	Woodcraft Hike	57
Thread the Needle	30	Woodcraft Signs	85
Three Around	88	Words from Words	25
Three in One	60		
Tie and Run	41	Yes or No	11
Torn Pictures	4		
Touch and Follow	29	Zigzag Bean Bag Relay	51
Tourist	24	Zigzag Circle Relay	52
Tower Football	34	Zoos	55

P. D. 10-42
1-46